Supercharge
Your Best Life.

Also by Scott Allan

Empower Your Thoughts

Empower Your Deep Focus

Rejection Reset

Rejection Free

Relaunch Your Life

Drive Your Destiny

The Discipline of Masters

Do the Hard Things First

Undefeated

Fail Big

Nothing Scares Me

No Punches Pulled

Supercharge Your Best Life

The Elite Performer's Framework

Optimal Peak Performance Strategies for Relentless Growth and Building a Bulletproof Lifestyle

Scott Allan

ISBN Paperback: 978-1-989599-68-6

ISBN eBook: 978-1-989599-67-9

ISBN Hardcover: 978-1-990484-19-3

CONTENTS

"Mastery, I learned, was not something genetic, or for a lucky few. It is something we can all attain if I get rid of some misconceptions and gain clarity as to the required path."

Robert Greene

Lessons in **Supercharging Your Best Life**

"There are two types of people who will tell you that you cannot make a difference in this world: those who are afraid to try and those who are afraid you will succeed."

Ray Goforth

Gary Keller, the author of one of my favorite books *The One Thing*, has said: ""Anyone who dreams of an uncommon life, eventually discovers there is no choice but to seek an uncommon approach to living it."

The foundations upon which I have lived, and everything I learn and teach, is centered around this obsessive drive to create an uncommon lifestyle. The journey has been a slow progression towards mastery and self-transcendence, fueled by stages of relentless growth. Through a life of success and repetitive failure, I have implemented the *Peak Performance Strategies* to build relentless growth opportunity, and engineer an environment centred around creating a limitless mindset.

In *Supercharge Your Best Life*, I will share with you the best strategies for habit development, creating an optimized goal system, visualizing the world you want to live in, and then, providing you with tools to construct that world.

Taking First Steps

This is the beginning of living the uncommon lifestyle. Doing the things that most people are not willing to do and confronting your fears when there is no other choice.

If you are stuck in life and don't know how to move ahead, I can help you.

If you have a desire to explore the unfolding mystery in this world and you aren't sure where to start, I can help you.

If you want to optimize your mindset and build a tangible reality from just your imagination, I can help you to achieve this. I can teach you the principles and framework for creating an extraordinary lifestyle.

You only have to **believe in the possibility**.

But before we begin, a few words about who I am, and what I do...

It Started Here...

You see, I grew up in a small town and a lot of people stay there. And while there is a great comfort in living near your parents and childhood friends, a pulsing, restless drive pushed me out the door towards an unknown destiny.

This journey has taken me around the world, and through countries and many cultures that I thought existed only in a dream. I have scuba dived to the depths of oceans and walked through temples sitting on top of broken foundations that were built thousands of years ago by people long forgotten. I walked for miles along the Great Wall, watched whales leap out of the water when nobody else was looking, and eaten food that still moved on the plate.

Over the years, I have had many adventures, immersed myself in culture and language, and danced on beaches in places whose names I don't remember. but the greatest discovery yet has been that of self-discovery.

This life has unfolded in ways I had never imagined, but the journey for us all begins as a small flicker in the dark that grows brighter with each step moving forward. As you discover the best of yourself, you become the best version of who you are meant to be.

It is this destiny that brings us together in this book *Supercharge Your Best Life*, and as the gaps of time close in on us all, we have this brief time together to build something magnificent and make a real difference. But the difference can only be measured by the impact of change you bring about in this world.

I have measured success over the years in many ways—financial gain, promotions, and collecting material things. But the greatest proof of success there is will always be the joy you bring into people's lives, and the healing ways of your soul from one person to the next.

This is a system of principles that build great things. There is no finish line in this life. There is only the here and the now and what you do with the moment. Your future is simply one moment of time stringing into the next just like links in a chain. So, the future is now, and your momentary actions and decisions create that future.

You are capable of amazing things, and by empowering your mind to push against resistance and break the fear holding you back, anything is possible.

I want you to succeed. I believe that you want the same thing, and it begins with a commitment to becoming the greatest version of yourself. Still hard to imagine? Close your eyes and visualize—for ten minutes—your life in the next five years.

How do you want it to unfold? What experiences do you visualize having? How is your dream going to be realized? By what code will you live by to supersede all your limitations and ascend to that next level that is waiting just around the bend?

"You can only fail if you fail yourself. By tapping into your hidden abilities and discovering what you are truly capable of, you become unstoppable. This is the

path to empowering your life, success, and everything in between."

There are many people who are waiting for things to just happen. They wait for someone to show them what to do, or who to be, or what to work on next; and as a result, many people end up living life based on the decisions other people are making.

The goal with *Supercharging Your Best Life* is to turn your vision—your dream—into a tangible lifestyle. In all of my work and teachings, everything is centered around clarity of purpose. Knowing what you want, and then, doing whatever it takes to makes it real.

I provide real-world action plans that get results through consistent action taking. I believe in results that are sustainable, measurable and fulfilling. It's not just about rah-rah and feeling good, but taking action and feeling great from the successful results and ultimately the outcome you want.

The strategies in this book are designed to take you from here to there. The "here" is where you begin from, and the "there" is where you imagine yourself arriving at. It is your road map to formulate a detailed blueprint that directs your focused attention in the right direction.

The foundations for building an extraordinary life lie within your imagination. It is your mission to open this door to all things possible. And believe me when I say, anything is possible.

These strategies are not quick-fix gimmicks or meant to transform your life in 30 days or less. But what I can promise you is, if you commit to change in the long-term and be patient with yourself as you work through this program, you will achieve amazing results. It may be slow at first, but progress is about moving forward.

If you have been feeling stuck for a long time, the strategies here are designed to get you unstuck and feeling great about your life. Even if you're already feeling great, you can take it to the next level. There is no such thing as a ceiling. We create our own limitations, and we can create a limitless mindset, too. And creating this mindset is something I'm super pumped about helping you to do.

Best Practice for Reading This Book

There are several ways you can learn from this book. You can pick a chapter and dive right in. Or work on the chapter for goal setting first. I've tested this book with over 500 readers and the majority voted to start from the beginning and work through each of the challenges one by one.

The pacing is really up to you. These strategies are the principles and values I have built my life around, and as tough as they can be, the strategies are meant to serve you for the long-term. I would suggest reading through the book once, and then after getting a feel for it, you can pick and choose your favorite strategies to practice more deeply.

The principles you will learn in *Supercharge Your Best Life* are:

(1) Supercharge Your **Master Mindset.** Learn the specific strategies for taking total charge of your mindset through intention, clarity and forming a growth mindset.

(2) Supercharge Your **Fearless Confidence:** Confidence begins with your decision to learn a new skill, change something about yourself, and being intentional about living differently. Confidence and taking massive action work together. Learn to beat your excuses and disable the self-doubt anchoring you to the past

(3) Supercharge Your **Positive Mental Attitude:** Your decisions, emotions, and the success you achieve depends heavily on your attitude toward the events and people influencing your thoughts.

(4) Supercharge Your **Visual Imagination.** One of the most powerful strategies for developing self-confidence and creating the life you want is mentally rehearsing the steps required to get you there. This is how concentrated visualization plays an important role in your success. When you can map out life's journey through your imagination, you are mentally rehearsing the actions needed to move straight to your goal.

(5) Supercharge Your **Self-Compassion.** Imagine what you could accomplish, where you could go, and who you could become if you had a level of compassion for yourself so deep that nothing could break it.

Self-compassion ties everything together. When you can embrace the importance you bring to this world, compassion begins with clarity of your mindful intent.

(6) Supercharge Your **Best Habits.** Bad habits are draining, but a system of good habits supported by a disciplined routine can defeat the habits holding you back. In this training on developing better habits, learn the framework for creating sustainable habits that support your goals and stacks your wins to achieve better results in the long run.

(7) Supercharge Your **Personal Growth:** Personal growth is the foundation of success. It is a commitment to continuously improve your life in the areas of mindset, spirituality, financial, intellectual, emotional, and physical health.

Learn the steps for investing in your personal growth and, begin to stack the building blocks that leads to creating an extraordinary life.

(8) Supercharge Your **Body.** Just as the mind requires mental nourishment to operate at peak effectiveness, the body requires a source of energy to function at its fullest capacity. When your body and mind are well-nourished, this contributes to the overall value and fulfillment found in each day.

(9) Supercharge Your **Goals.** Your goals provide you with a sense of direction and are the blueprints to construct the reality of your dreams.

By creating a system of goals that inspire and motivate you to engage in positive action, you plant the roots of success and design a system for success that brings every opportunity imaginable.

(10) Supercharge Your **Emotions.** The ability to change your state of mind is the most powerful strategy you can implement. The one reason people are so unhappy is because they are stuck in a state of mind that is creating negative emotions. In order to master your emotional state, you will have to start with bringing your thoughts into the present moment.

(11) Supercharge Your **Resilience.** Resilience is the process of adapting well in the face of adversity, trauma, tragedy, threats, or significant sources of stress", such as family and relationship problems, health issues, or a financial crisis.

By mastering the art of resilience, you can bounce back from difficult experiences and learn from past trials and failure.

(12) Supercharge Your **Focus.** Deep Focus is about managing mental energy, and directing your thoughts into a laser-focused stream, while ignoring the multitude of distractions competing for your attention. In this training, you will learn how to manage **focus** and declutter your mind (and environment) for creating a quality of life that allows for higher levels of creativity.

(13) Supercharge Your **Beliefs.** Beliefs play a pivotal role in shaping the course of your life. When your old beliefs

fail you, it's time to take intentional action and create a new story for yourself. In this training, learn the six steps you can take to begin changing anything in your life.

Structuring Your Roadmap to Building a Great Life

Join me on this journey as I walk you through each of the strategies here and how you can apply this blueprint to your own life.

Becoming successful isn't a once-in-a-lifetime-event. In every case for anyone that has achieved success, it is a series of milestones that one achieves on the journey.

No matter where you are at on your journey, you can start from today, to turn your passion into something amazing. I believe you are here for a reason, and that we are going to help each other on the path towards greatness and creating an extraordinary lifestyle.

The only thing you have to do is begin.

Take that first step now, and begin where you are, with what you have, with who you are.

You are enough to start today.

Scott A

"The only thing worse than starting something and failing is...not starting something."

— Seth Godin

Supercharge Your
Master Mindset

"If you are facing a new challenge or being asked to do something that you have never done before don't be afraid to step out. You have more capability than you think you do but you will never see it unless you place a demand on yourself for more."

— **Joyce Meyer**

Your mindset is your own.

As Viktor Frankl said, "Everything can be taken from a man but one thing, the last of human freedoms: To choose one's attitude in any given set of circumstances, to choose one's own way."

People who can, believe they can. People who don't or won't—even if they want it—will never get what they desire, because they don't believe. You must believe you can, or else you won't.

Your mindset is a choice.

You are living in one of two worlds: a growth mindset, or a fixed mindset. For optimum performance and living into your greatness, you must direct your thoughts towards a growth mindset.

A growth mindset is built on the foundations that achievement and failure come largely from effort, a commitment to learning and constant and never-ending development.

A fixed mindset is built from the opposite point of view. In a fixed mindset, you believe that mental traits are inborn and remain unchangeable, limiting what you can learn, do, be, and achieve. You have no hope of becoming better because this is "the way it is" and I can't change it.

The story you tell yourself is the script that defines your success or failure. Even if you're not aware of it, your subconscious voice and the thoughts you create are communicating messages to your brain that defines in visual detail what is possible. You create the realm of possibility (and impossibility) in your mind. Your limitations are guided by the mindset of either I can or I can't. I believe or I don't believe. I will or I won't.

Be aware of the lies you create. They are deceptive and emerge from a place you that builds fear, doubt and uncertainty. These are the three enemies of a growth mindset. Henry Ford was right when he said, "Whether you think you can, or you think you can't – you're right," emphasizes how much attitude determines success or failure. Your attitude is a building block for mindset.

How often do you say to yourself or people, "I can't..." and then fill in the blank? Yes, there are many things we can't do... yet. If I want to play a sport but have never tried, I can start to play and develop the skills with practice. If you want to play guitar but it's been thirty years since you picked it up, you can still learn.

Be careful when you use negative parallels such as "Oh yeah, I used to do that." The past is a funnel of experiences we frame as either successful or failures. If I invested money in something and lost, I failed and might never try that again. Your mindset states: "That didn't work. Don't try it again."

Your mindset is a choice.

We all have conditioned limitations. Someone once told me I had no musical talent. Those words stuck with me, and I stayed away from anything that was musical. I believed it at the time. When someone asked if I played something, I said, "No, I'm not very good at music." However, that wasn't true. I believe I was good at music. I would write songs, even without knowing the notes. I'd come up with lyrics and pass them on to other musicians.

By telling people you can't do something, it reinforces your failure. What you say is what you do. Growing up, I defeated myself continuously by reinforcing the belief that "I can't."

Limitations are built on past failures or shortcomings, and your limits define who you are, what you can do, and the actions you take. This is true for most things: The amount of money you make; the work you do, the people you spend time with, and how you spend time when alone.

Your world is a mirrored reflection of the mindset you are invested in building. Circumstances have very little to do with it. We are influenced by environment, but you can manipulate your conditions to work for you instead of against you. In the end, it is your decisions that decide your path. What choices are you making right now that will lead your life tomorrow?

Your mindset is intentional.

Make your growth mindset an intentional action, and anything you desire is yours. Let others make that decision for you, and this gives up your freedom to create, experiment, and experience a life that is your own. You will fall into the trap of structuring a fixed mindset based on the expectations according to others.

If you want to predict your future, take control of your thoughts. Your thoughts—when used in positive ways—are powerful tools to expand your mindset. Negative thoughts can be tools to damage your mindset and guarantees failure.

Take control of your mind at the start of each day. Do this first thing when you awaken before negative thoughts can take hold. Before you go to sleep, spend fifteen minutes meditating and thinking deeply about your future. Visualize how you want your world to be created.

Be intentional with your goals. Take responsibility for your life's journey and feed your growth mindset with wisdom, philosophy and positive affirmations. It's hungry and it is wants everything you can give it. The ability to fix on this daily habit is the cornerstone of success or failure.

"No matter what, people grow. If you chose not to grow, you're staying in a small box with a small mindset. People who win go outside of that box. It's very simple when you look at it."

— Kevin Hart

Believing in your limitations gives them power over you. By reinforcing this mindset, you are pushing yourself into a corner of limited possibilities. Take an imaginary line and draw it down the center of your mind. On one side is all the greatness you aspire to be. Your life is filled with abundance.

You visualize the world as you want to live in it. This could be your life as a successful business owner, a mediation expert, or a motivational speaker that is changing the lives of thousands. Or, you're creating a positive, love-rich environment for your family to grow and develop in.

Your mindset and attitude are contagious, and the people around you will be influenced by you in more ways than you can imagine. You decide the world you want to live in, and then set your focus on making it happen. You are alive and thriving with energy because you know that the journey and possibilities are endless and unlimited.

On the other side of this imaginary line is your fixed mindset. In this realm, you continue to live the same way you always have, not because you want to but, you think there is no choice. You were brought up this way, trained to think that you have little worth or value. You buy into these lies and it defines your world. With a fixed mindset, your thoughts are caught in an endless loop of negativity, excuses, scarcity and

In fact, it only takes one limiting belief to corrupt your success in life. One negative belief about who you are, your abilities, and what is possible for you, can carve out a lifetime of living within the confines of limited potential and wretched poverty.

I am talking about poverty of the mind, in which you become so poor intellectually that you fail to make forward progress in your life. Like a train stuck on the tracks due to bad weather conditions, your mind is stuck in neutral without momentum to push it forward. You are so poor in positive thinking and stuck in repetitive thoughts of past failures and dreams that failed to come true, you face defeat every day... and feel powerless to do anything about it.

A fixed mindset is the place where weeds have taken over your mind. Now, the solution is to do something about it. Is this how you want to live your life? Do you enjoy being trapped in this hell, believing your life is out of your hands, you have no choice, and that the future in twenty years is the same as it is now?

By buying into your fixed mindset, and the mindset of "I can't," you are sealing your own fate. You are determining your own worth. You are setting the future in stone. You are choosing to be less-than, instead of more-than. The fixed mindset revokes challenges and takes the easy way out. It is focused on existing in a realm of comfort, while avoiding difficulties.

Not a chance. You are the master gardener of your life. Imagine taking this line in your mind and moving it over the fixed mindset. I want you to visualize taking an eraser and wiping out all this garbage.

Imagine that you're a stage director, and when you arrive on the set, everything you see is all the wrong props. You get to work, clearing the stage right away until nothing is left but a clean floor. Now you can bring in the pieces you want. You can build a new scene. You can set up a different reality for the actors. You can set the stage for a new reality.

Wipe your mind clean. Reset your day, reset the moment. Take command of your mind. A growth mindset is a place for change, transformation, and invention. This is where creators, shakers, and people who build the impossible thrive. The garden of your mind is your playground, and you decide the games to play.

If you feel trapped, helpless, limited, or poor, it is because you're living your life from the perspective of a fixed mindset. If you're trapped, you can get unstuck. You can walk out of that place. Are you certain you can't do something? You most likely can, when you switch from a fixed to a growth mindset.

In Carol S. Dweck's bestselling book *Mindset*, she says:

"In a fixed mindset, people believe their qualities are fixed traits and therefore cannot change. ... According to Dweck, when a student has a fixed mindset, they believe that their basic abilies, intelligence, and talents are fixed traits. They think that you are born with a certain amount and that's all you have."

Imagine what you will be able to do when you stop saying, "I can't," and begin to say, "Yes, I can!" Just repeating these words empowers your mind to believe them.

You must believe to achieve.

Do you think you can't find a partner to love you and spend time with you? Yes, you can!

Do you think you can't speak in front of people because you have never tried this before? You can do this!

Do you think you can't earn a million dollars this year because you never finished college? Yes, you can earn a million, or ten million.

Do you think you can't change your life because this is the way things are, and now, you have to live with it? Lies. Not true. Yes, you can change anything about your life, starting today.

Yes, you've got this!

Yes, your expectations for the future are what fix you to the outcomes. You can predict your life and how it is going to be for the next 20 years by taking a serious look at how you are living now.

Your goal is to stretch yourself—one step at a time—so that you move closer to developing your growth mindset. It is there, waiting for you to do something. Your mind is engineered to become a learning center. The mind wants to explore, grow, and be driven to the boundaries of unlimited potential.

We were not designed to stay behind a desk, lowering ourselves to standards set by others. You decide your worth and bring yourself to rise to that level.

You are standing on the edge of greatness. You are that greatness.

When you make a shift in your mindset, your thought patterns open up and you create a positive funnel for lasting change.

How is that for thinking highly of yourself? From now on, from today, from this moment, you can.

Now, here are three strategies you can develop today to create your "I can" mindset:

1. Put an end to your "I can't" psychology.

Here is what you should do: Take a count of how many times a day you refuse to do or accept anything because you say, "I can't do that." It is a habit we acquired at some point in the past, when we lost confidence in our real selves. It may have evolved in school, such as, "I can't do math," or "I can't play basketball." Now, maybe you really need more practice at these things. Not everyone can play basketball—no matter how hard they try—but whether you can or can't, it doesn't matter.

By building this phrase into your mindset, you start using it for everything that is challenging. In fact, saying, "I can't do something" becomes an easy cop-out. Before you know it, you are using it not just for what you can't do, but what you don't want to do. It becomes your default response.

Use "I can" when you feel you are about to resist something. For years, they were so many things I said I couldn't do, but I didn't want to do them because learning a new skill takes time and effort—two things I wasn't willing to invest.

Here are a few examples:

- "I can't cook." Well cooking isn't that difficult. I wasn't making gourmet meals, but I could cook basic food.

- "I can't save money." True, this was always challenging for me, but saving became easier when I switched my habit of spending to saving instead. Learning to invest and scale up is something I was never good at, but over time, I learned to save bigtime. In fact, I saved myself out of debt. Anyone can save cash if they learn a few basic skills and implement new saving habits.

- "I can't quit my day job." As it turns out, I could. I was just refusing to give it up because I was afraid of what would happen. When I realized that yes, I can quit this job and get something better, I took the necessary steps and made it happen.

Not being able to do something and convincing yourself you can't are two different things. I can't is a limiting function that steals your life away over time. I can't will defeat you before you attempt anything, and it keeps you scared because you never rise to the challenge.

Now, you know you can, and you will. The more focused your I can power becomes, the bigger your confidence will grow.

2. Train Your Brain to Think Big (but don't expect instant results). A lot of people I work with on mindset training begin with the best of intentions. But they fail after several weeks and revert back to the way things were. Why does this happen? We want instant results.

There are lots of messages out there claiming you can change in an instant, you can transform your state right now. Yes, you can change your mind right now...but five minutes later it creeps back into the cave you have been living in.

Change takes time, and the amount of time it takes depends. But that is not important. You must be on constant guard against the enemies of your mind. Think of your mindset as a fortress. Your fortress is surrounded by a great wall. This wall is protecting your precious assets from becoming corrupted by the enemy of past trauma, negative thoughts, and self-imposed limitations.

Every day is a battleground, and you are at WAR. This is how a mindset is forged. By thinking BIG and letting this scare you.

Make a decision every morning that you are going to win this fight. Take your stand. Your path to being extraordinary is on the other side of all your fears. You don't have to become great; you already are. You need to awaken to this and when you become aware of it, fight to protect it. The rest of the strategies in this book will show you exactly how to do that.

3. Move out of the past and lean into the present.

You can reframe your past experiences to view your life in a different way. View everything that happened in your life as a learning curve. Whatever it is that you are holding onto, realize that you did the best with what you had at that time. It couldn't have been any different than what it was. By doing this, you release the tension from inside your body. You can let go of worry. You can forgive yourself for not measuring up.

You made it. You're here. You are in this moment, and the present moment is the only place that matters. You can control this day.

I am not suggesting you forget about the past. That would be unrealistic. Frame your life as an incredible journey full of all incredible experiences. All the people in your life are part of the story, and you are the master storyteller

By framing your past experience as a necessary path to bring you here, you can let go of your old thoughts and failed expectations.

Now that you know how to supercharge your mindset, let's take a look at how to Supercharge Your mindset with a clear and committed decision.

"Always go with the choice that scares you the most, because that's the one that is going to help you grow."

— Caroline Myss

Your decisions are the driving force to attracting what you want into your life. When you make a clear, concrete decision about a career choice, a relationship, or a goal, it makes this materialize for you.

A decision is the switch that sets your mindset to take intentional action. A clear and definitive decision is the ignition switch for take-off. The moment your decision is made, massive action is determined to take place next.

Why We Make Irrational Decisions

One of the core reasons we make "bad" decisions—a decision that resulted in an undesirable outcome—is a lack of clarity around what you really wanted. But there are no guarantees that your decision is going to work out with your best intentions in mind.

You make a decision to invest $10,000 in a new product and it goes bust. You lose $10k.

You make a decision to take a great job opportunity with another company and quit your full-time job. Six months later that company goes bust. You are now unemployed.

You make a decision to marry the person of your dreams because things are going great and you're in love. Five years later they fall in love with someone else leaving you alone and rejected.

Were these bad decisions? Did you fail? Will you live the rest of your life with regret wishing you had made a different decision?

Let's be clear. If you decide to do nothing, make no decisions, take no action, and feign no risk...nothing happens. Or worse, you live life by default.

We make thousands of decisions every week, including what to eat, where to go, what clothes to wear, or who to spend time with. Other critical choices to make might include which university to attend, what courses to take online, when to change jobs or who to marry. These decisions are setting the stage for your journey moving forward.

Now, a real decision isn't just a lofty wish or a dream. If you say, "I want to earn ten thousand dollars per month doing what I love," while that sounds impressive, you need a strategy to achieve this. You also need a powerful WHY for making this your reality.

We all "want" things. We want to be healthier, earn more money, and spend more time with friends and family. But wanting it and deciding you're going to definitely have it are two separate realities.

Everything depends on your ability to decide what you want. It's about developing an umbrella plan in which you can envision the plan as a whole. The details come later, but every decision you make has to be followed by immediate action.

You can't get where you want to be if you don't know exactly where that is. It sounds like a simple concept, but many are lost on the journey because they haven't decided where they want to arrive someday.

People fail to decide what they want, then fail to commit to any course of action. And believe me when I say, that "someday" you talk about will be here before you know it. The best time to make a decision that changes your behavior was yesterday. The next best time is today.

Make a firm decision about what you want to accomplish, the values you are choosing to live by, and the principles to guide you to where you need to be. Focus all your attention on achieving whatever would have the greatest impact on what matters most to you.

Here is my **simple 6-step process for making decisions** and following through specific action to build momentum:

1. Make your decision. This is based on your long-term objective. Small decisions made daily contribute to overall success.

2. Internalize your decision. Is the best decision now? Is it in line with your long-term plan?

3. Commit yourself 100%. Now that you've made your decision, define your plan of action. Decide on one action step each day.

4. Learn and stay flexible. Not every decision will lead to a desired outcome. You are allowed to fail. Give yourself permission to make mistakes and try again.

5. Make decision-making a consistent habit. Practice leads to progress. Continue to make decisions that shape the force of your life.

6. Let go of the outcome. Don't become obsessed about the end result. Take a moment to make the decision that you've been struggling with the most. Then, focus on the actions that will take you straight to your goal.

- Today, decide on something that you have been avoiding. This could be a decision that changes the way you eat, think, or how you control your behavior. Your decision might be something you have to discuss first with your partner or children.

- After making this decision—even if it scares you— stick with it and follow through with your first course of action.

Create a goal for yourself to make one important decision per day and then, follow through with the first action step.

Supercharge Your
Fearless Confidence

"Limitations live only in our minds. But if we use our imaginations, our possibilities become limitless."

— Jamie Paolinetti

Confidence is a state of mind that you can elevate at will. But I've met many people who would say, "I'll do it when I'm feeling more confident" or "I don't have what it takes" or "I'd do it but the fear is holding you back." I know what this feels like because I've been there many times.

I used to think confidence was a magic genie that was someday going to show up and give me the courage to take fearless action. I would watch other people succeed at a level I wasn't even close to and I would think, "How do they do that and make it look easy?"

When I had this discussion with one of my mentors, who has created a million-dollar business, he said: "I'm just as scared as everyone else. But when your passion and obsession are screaming at you to act, you do it anyway. The confidence came later."

That was when I realized the secret to being confident. Like most people, I was waiting for confidence to show up and deliver the courage to make me great. I waited a long time, and nothing happened. So I got busy anyway. And guess what happened? My confidence began to grow stronger. Another description for confidence is this:

"Confidence means trusting oneself, having complete faith in any task and letting go the fear of failure. People with a high level of self-confidence achieve their desired goals in life and attain success."

Confidence is about faith, belief and trusting yourself. It doesn't mean you won't fail, but knowing you can fail, giving yourself permission to make mistakes, and knowing that you will make it. If you do nothing and wait for courage, you will never know what you are capable of. It's not about what you can do now, but the willingness to learn as you push forward.

If you want to climb the mountain but you've never tried it before, you will find a way to get to the top. Your confidence is built into determination that there is a way to get there, and you will find it.

You're not born with confidence. It is an innate ability that can be built through learning, trying and failing, and overcoming challenges and obstacles. Think about the first time you tried anything. You had no idea what you were doing, but you continued to push ahead until you succeeded. There are times we give up, too. This doesn't mean you failed but decided now is not the time. You can always return to it later if it means that much to you.

I didn't learn to swim until I was 26 years old. I was terrified of the water and couldn't swim. I didn't have any confidence in my ability to learn, either. But a friend of mine convinced me to take swimming lessons for three months because she couldn't swim either, but she's always wanted to participate in a swimming competition. Well, in the first week I was hopeless. I couldn't even tread water. One month later I was doing the front crawl, it wasn't great, but I was moving through the water.

That was when I had a shift in mindset. Something happened inside, and then I started to believe it was possible. If I could learn this in one month, what else was possible? The butterfly? In the second month I was doing that, too. After three months, I was able to tread water, do the front crawl, and could swim 100 meters. My confidence in the water was unbreakable.

Fast forward five years later and I was scuba diving in Palau at 40 meters depth looking for WW2 wrecks. Would I have taken up diving if I couldn't even tread water? Would I have had the confidence to get on a boat or put on a scuba outfit? Not a chance. Since then I've done over 300 dives in six countries and have seen sharks, whales, Moray Eels, and seen old wrecks at the bottom of the ocean that I once would have had to look in books to see. This all happened because I decided to take swimming lessons.

Confidence begins with your decision to learn a new skill, change something about yourself, and being intentional about living differently. Nothing happens when you do nothing. Confidence and action work together.

I'll give you one more example. You're learning from this book right now because I wrote it. But in the beginning—going back ten years ago—I was only dreaming of being a writer. I talked about it all the time, read books on how to write, and yet, when I sat down to it it scared me. What if I suck as a writer? What if nobody reads my work? What if I fail and then prove to myself that it really is a pipedream that will never happen?

I had to turn off the self-doubt, push it aside, and learn to write badly. Like the swimming lessons, I was hopeless in the beginning. But I noticed several months later that it was getting better. So I kept up with it, and within one year, I had a badly written manuscript of about 60,000 words. My confidence as a writer had improved by 100x from last year. My beliefs had shifted. I was now confident that this was possible. I wanted to publish the book but how do you do that? Writing is one thing, but publishing?

One lesson you will learn as you build your own confidence and work towards a goal that matters. You will start from the bottom and work hard in the beginning. You will want to give up but if you keep moving ahead, like the climber on that mountain, you'll hit the mid-way point. You now have 2 paths to take.

You can give up and go back down the way you came, pack up and go home. Or...

Push to the summit. This is the pinnacle point when fearless confidence is forged. In the moment when you decide you will complete the journey. When there are two voices inside your head. One is telling you—and yelling at you—to quit and go back the way you came.

"What were you thinking? Are you insane? You don't need this pressure?" It is the voice of fear and failure.

The other voice is strong but silent. It is asking you only one thing: "If you give up now, what else is there?"

You can always go back to the couch and watch TV. Or you can get out there and make a difference. Your fearless confidence is forged in the moments when you face your fear and do it anyway.

Confidence isn't about what you can do. It's what you are willing to do to get to where you want to be mentally, physically, or spiritually. It's choosing to be great even if you have no idea what that means or how to make it happen. There is no such thing as a perfect plan. Decide your next step. What will it take to begin?

Do you have to sign up for a class? Pick up a pen? Make a phone call? Buy a book or course?

Take that first step on the mountain. Then take one more. Keep moving. Excuses will try to stop you. Your mind will fill with self-doubt. You will even question your sanity as to why you're trying this.

"If you hear a voice within you say 'you cannot paint,' then by all means paint, and that voice will be silenced."

— Vincent Van Gogh

Making excuses is your mind's way of deceiving you. Filled with the sounds of self-pity and limited reasoning, an excuse is very convincing.

Your excuses sound like this:

· "I am too old for this."

· "It didn't work for my friends, so why should it work for me?"

· "I'll wait until someone else does it and I know it works."

· "I don't have any natural ability."

Eliminate your excuses. By erasing this negative self-talk from your mind, you align your mindset with the best decision to take intentional action.

Fear can only control you when you allow it to.

Make a list of your excuses that stop you from pushing forward. What's holding you back from living the life you truly want? Refer to the first step in this module and "Begin Where You Are" by implementing the simplest task possible.

Do something. Get creative, get active and move. Doubt loves the passive mind that falls into the worry trap. It feeds off your fears and worry. Don't feed your self-doubt, but rather, starve it.

Doubt is a term that describes a lack of trust in oneself. Confidence is the opposite of doubt. It's the unbreakable faith that anything is possible. Most people fail, not from lack of ability but, a lack of trust in who they are truly capable of becoming.

You don't have to wait for confidence to show up before you do something that scares you. You don't need courage before you act; you gain confidence after you overcome your greatest moments of doubt. Confidence is like motivation; if we wait depend on its arrival, we could spend a lifetime waiting.

Self-doubt is always temporary. As soon as you get out there and do it, it's diminished. Remember my story about learning to swim? In the beginning I couldn't tread water. Five years later I was at the bottom of the ocean.

I still have fears that hold me back to this day. Although I've written over twenty books, there are days when I question my skills as a writer, a creator, and as an educator. The fear of failure is always there. But so is the belief that anything is possible. At the end of the day, it is the fear you feed that grows stronger.

There are no guarantees in this life. If you're waiting for a guarantee before you take that leap, you'll be waiting until the end of your life. You will die with regret and there is nothing worse than this. I'm not afraid of dying, but I am afraid of getting to the end of my life and realizing I didn't pursue my vision. I won't settle for what I can get, and neither should you.

Go after what you want. Don't just follow your dreams, but lead your life with your dreams at the top of that summit as it pulls you forward.

Confidence is the other side of living in fear. People who exist in a permanent state of fear are holding themselves back from doing. They think that they're going to lose out somehow. They doubt all ability to succeed.

You can build your confidence up by taking fearless action now. Kill your doubt before it kills your dreams. If there's something you're dying to do with your life, and you're being held back, remember that you're not going to live forever.

Make the most of the day. Jump in and start swimming even if you can't! It's a better alternative than regretting the things you never did.

Fearless Confidence and Breaking the Fear of Rejection

1. Rejection is about you, not them.

One of the greatest illusions about rejection is that we convince ourselves we are being personally "rejected," as if someone is doing something to us. But in fact, the rejection begins on the inside. This can be traced back to your inner critics, those old voices that tell you, "You're no good," or "Why bother? You'll just fail anyway."

When we reject ourselves first, we are sending a clear message to people. It is like putting the writing on the wall yourself. People can sense when someone is lacking confidence. If you walk into a bank to get a loan and you believe—even before you meet with the loans officer—that there's no way you'll get the loan, this feeling carries with you. Be aware of situations in which you're rejecting yourself before anyone else gets a chance to.

2. Stop blaming external forces for failed results.

Taking full responsibility for your life and current situation is a powerful character-building step. By taking charge, you take control. Deciding to stop blaming others for your unhappiness is taking a healthy approach to being responsible. This doesn't mean you have to forget what happened in the past, but you do have to move on from it.

This can only happen when you choose to live life on your terms by making a firm decision and following through with action to create a positive and fulfilling future. You are giving yourself permission to be free. Nobody else will give that to you. Once you accept your life as it is and are willing to do whatever it takes to move forward, then you are ready to be responsible.

Practice forgiveness, acceptance, and commit to moving forward. Don't stay stuck in one spot, waiting for someone else to make it all better. When you wait for someone else to take charge, you lose the chance to make the situation better and the opportunity to heal yourself is gone.

3. Take an opinion as a biased lack of knowledge.

Everyone has an opinion. It is one of the ways we communicate our thoughts and emotions. We formulate opinions about each other based on what is said, actions taken, or differences in personality. If you struggle with rejection, then varying opinions can have a negative impact on your confidence.

We take the opinions and judgments from others as a personal insult. If someone doesn't like the way you look or dress, or they don't like your attitude and the way you carry yourself, you may take this too personally. There are many details other people use to construct an opinion about you as a person.

It is easy to believe everything you hear, especially if you are hypersensitive. Even though we can't stop the world from having opinions, we can choose how to accept it. Will you retaliate and come back with your own attack? Or will you take what is said as a biased remark based on lack of evidence? Besides, who really knows you better than yourself? Why should you take someone else's word as the only truth when you know it just isn't so?

This works the other way, too. Your evaluation of another person is based on the same lack of information that others use to construct their opinions about you. You have two choices here: You can continue the negative cycle of labeling others just as they label you, or you can practice total acceptance as a strategy to build more empathy toward others.

A lack of empathy is at the core of many social problems. When we buy in to the opinions and criticisms of strangers, we believe what they decide is the truth about us. But it's not. Rarely are first opinions correct.

4. Revisit your shame-based childhood.

For most people, living in rejection has its roots in early childhood. Back then, we were treated without the attention or respect we deserved. Criticism was rampant. We were never good enough, no matter how hard we tried or what level of success we could achieve. This resulted in a life of living in shame, a core attribute of those who feel rejected.

It can be a painful experience to revisit this period of our lives when not everything was perfect. But by returning to that particular event in your past when you were most vulnerable, and by walking yourself through that pain again, in time you can mend the damage that was inflicted.

5. Let go of the past failures that define you.

If you were rejected in the past, you'll reject yourself in the future. We replay old stories of failures and negative results from our past. When this happens, we create more of the same. Your past is not who you are; it is who you were. Are you the same person you were twenty years ago? I know I'm not.

Sure, many things about you haven't changed and people still refer to you as someone they know based on a lifetime of friendship. But we are all evolving even if those changes are subtle. Basing your future happiness or success on what you got in the past is a way to repeat history.

You can define your future by the actions you take now. Your thoughts, words, and emotions are powerful and can change your life in a moment if conditioned properly.

6. Practice getting rejected on purpose.

In his bestselling book, Rejection Proof, Jia Jiang takes on a massive challenge. He set out to get rejected over the course of 100 days in a project he dubbed <u>100 Days of Rejection.</u>

During this social experiment, Jia would try outrageous stunts of courage to push his fear of rejection beyond anything he had ever experienced. He would ask for Olympic symbol donuts, give $5 to five random people, and challenge a CEO to a staring contest. His purpose was to desensitize himself to rejection so that he could overcome his fears in order to live his dream as an entrepreneur.

So, how about you? In what ways could you put yourself out there and get rejected in order to numb yourself to the fear? We put more effort into avoiding fear than encouraging it. So, when rejection happens (and it will) it hurts and we remember the pain as something we'd rather not repeat. As a result, we stay away from it as much as possible.

7. Build your confidence through consistent practice.

The way to build confidence is to take consistent and intentional action. Challenge yourself to do the things that are difficult. These are easy to spot because we resist what we don't want to do. Or we put off difficult tasks because they are hard but actually carry the greatest rewards in the long run.

Confidence is an "action building" activity. It can only be built when we put our fears and uncertainties to the test.

Maximize Your Confidence:
20-Point Fearless Confidence Cheat Sheet

1. Take action on the one thing you are resisting.
2. Make a list of abilities that you are good at.
3. Identify the one thing you feel you are better at than anybody else you know.
4. Develop patience with your learning process.
5. Take one positive action a day toward helping another person.
6. Prepare an action list of your goals for each week. Keep this list visible at all times.
7. Walk with your head up. Don't stare at the ground when you are walking.
8. Focus on one bad habit and change it. Start small and work your way toward changing bigger habits that aren't working.
9. Make a gratitude list of things you are happy about.
10. De-clutter your home. Start in each room and move through the house.
11. De-clutter your mind for ten minutes a day. Do short meditation sessions of ten minutes each.
12. Work on a new skill. Set aside a "learning time" for this and schedule yourself for a daily training session. This works best when you schedule it.
13. Tackle one task that you have been putting off. Set up a timer and work on it for twenty-minute increments.

14. Approach someone you don't know and strike up a conversation. Compliment them on something or just ask how they are doing. You can do this with someone you haven't spoken to in a long while, too.

15. Read a positive book on self-development. Two of my favorites are *The One Thing* by Gary Keller and *The 7 Habits of Highly Effective People* by Stephen Covey. Set aside twenty minutes per day for reading.

16. Eliminate the source of negative energy that's draining your confidence. Is it a person? A negative behavior? Work on pushing it away from your life and align everything with positive actions.

17. Create a wall collage of your goals, dreams, and aspirations. Include places you desire to visit, and challenges you plan to take on.

18. Create multiple income streams to boost your monthly income. Making more money is a major confidence booster. It adds to the joy and freedom of your lifestyle.

19. Join a mastermind group or hire a life coach. Meet up regularly and discuss your confidence building strategies.

20. Embrace the things you fail at. Visualize achieving a level of success that seems impossible and work toward it. Include this in your wall collage

Supercharge Your **PMA** **(Positive Mental Attitude)**

"If you have a positive attitude and constantly strive to give your best effort, eventually you will overcome your immediate problems and find you are ready for greater challenges."

— Pat Riley

Your decisions, emotions, and the success you achieve depends heavily on your attitude toward the events and people influencing your thoughts. The success of everything you work towards depends largely on a positive mental attitude.

Strategies for Creating a Positive Attitude

Here are the strategies for building and maintaining a positive attitude that will change the course of your life.

Stay connected with your thoughts. Observe what is happening with your thinking, and then start to make slight adjustments. This won't happen instantly. And even for people who are highly positive, creative, and successful, they, too, must constantly change direction when necessary.

A positive mental attitude is not a goal to achieve. It is a state of mind you must work your way into, and then maintain with direct action, affirmations and building good habits into your routine. Just as a garden is never truly rid of its weeds because new ones crop up, your mind needs constant attention, too.

How will you stay connected with your thoughts? For example, you can read your best ten affirmations or quotes first thing in the morning.

Pay attention. When a negative thought creeps in, take charge of your mind right then and there. Interrupt the thought instead of letting your thoughts run rampant. Tell your mind, "I'm not thinking about that!" Cut the negative lies in half before they have a chance to dig in. Do not give your negative voice power. Take charge of your life and replace this negative carnage with a positive action.

Here are suggestions for taking charge of your Positive Mental Attitude:

- Focus on what you love to do and start doing it.

- Leave your failures outside of your mind. Keep them as reminders and lessons learned but they are not your future.

- Get a mentor or accountability partner. Learn from this person and do what they have done.

- Make "Affirmation Repetition" a habit. Have a list of affirmations or quotes you can read at the start of every day. Check the back of this book for affirmation suggestions.

- Do one act of kindness at least once a day.

- Spend 30 minutes with your thoughts every evening. This means turning off all devices, the TV, and shutting yourself away for 30 minutes. This doesn't mean you have to meditate, but just be one with your thoughts.

- A defeat is not a loss; life is not all a streak of wins. You will stumble and fall. Get back up and try it again. Persistence is a major positive skill that is going to give you a huge PMA if you keep it up.

- Write down one thing you are grateful for every day. Do this as soon as you wake up. It will take 10 seconds. Just one thing. Keep a gratitude list. I started to keep one two years ago. I write down one thing every morning or at night that I am grateful for.

- Don't rely on things for your happiness or fulfillment.

- Nobody can make you feel miserable or sad; that is a choice.

- Avoid making time for people who like to waste yours.

- Believe that freedom is your choice; you can either free your mind or keep it enslaved with negative thoughts and images. Would you rather be free or be a slave to your alternative self?

What lessons have you learned? You can add them to this list to remind you of what you can do and to see how far you have come.

Now that we have the essential elements to create your attitude, what are you going to do with it?

Optimistic About the Future

Optimism is a powerful motivator. Optimistic people are focused on making the future as bright as possible. They are not pulled into events in the past that are over and can never be changed. They move on and scale up.

Optimistic people talk about all the great things they are going to do, and whom they plan to do it with. How about you? What is your level of optimism?

Let go of thoughts that don't make you strong.

When you take on the attitude of a person with an optimistic outlook, you are saying no to the thoughts that could potentially hold you back; thoughts of worry, anxiety, and self-defeat are no longer entertained.

Optimism generates its own positive force. You don't need any help from the outside when you take on the role of an optimistic adventurer. The world is yours if you aren't afraid to stand up and take it.

How will you use optimism to build your next adventure?

Clarity of Life Mission/Believe in the Journey

Clarity in your life is a deeper knowing of what you want, and a willingness to do anything to get it. You are saying to the world, "I am ready to accept anything that you have—good or bad. Bring it on."

The road of this journey is not without its challenges. There will be good times and bad times; failures and successes; gains and losses. But if you are clear about why you are doing what you are doing, and you stay focused on the path you have chosen; the outcome is not important.

Believe in the power of your thoughts.

You can only control what you can control, and in most situations in life, that means very little outside of yourself. Stick with your life mission, and if you aren't sure what that is, do what you feel is right in your heart.

Don't wait for someone else to show up and teach you how it's done. Know what to do by clarifying the actions and goals you need to get this thing done.

What is your next action going to be?

Building Positive Habits That Reinforce Your Positive Attitude

When it comes to being successful at anything, you'll always find a person's habits are at the core of their success. But not just any habits. You need a system of positive habits that support you and help you build your goals.

For example:

- Waking up early and working out for 30 minutes is a positive habit. It gets you into shape and makes you feel great.

- Writing a book requires you to sit down any write a certain amount of words for a set amount of days until the book is finished.

- Training for a full marathon is about working up to running the pace and being able to complete the marathon, which is about 43 kilometers (i.e., 26.2 miles).

These are habits that you act on every day. When you wake up your mind to act on your thoughts, you can do anything. In addition, it feeds into your positive mindset. You're feeling great about waking up early and training!

Talk Incessantly About Your Goals

When you have a goal that gets you up early in the morning and fires you up right away, you feel great about your life. Did you know that most people walking around have no goals? If you don't have a goal to shoot for, it impacts your attitude. You are more susceptible to moodiness, negative thinking, and are reacting to circumstances instead of creating them.

If you haven't yet taken the time to craft out your life for the next five years, do it right now. If you already know what you want, but you're holding back for fear of failure, the time is now to break this fear and work on what you really want. Nobody is going to show up and just hand you your life. You must reach out and grab it.

"In every day, there are 1,440 minutes. That means we have 1,440 daily opportunities to make a positive impact."

— Les Brown

Once you know what you want, start to talk about it. Tell everyone. Do you want to travel the world and see places you only dreamed of? Talk about it. People may not believe you at first but telling everyone about it sets these goals on fire. It molds your attitude into a funnel of action.

It solidifies your positive attitude by making you more energized and focused on future events. You won't have time to focus on the past and get caught up in old trifles because you'll be too focused on building your future. Your confidence will peak to an all-new level, and you'll give off positive energy everywhere you go.

Take Responsibility for your Life (and Everything Happening in It)

Accepting responsibility for your own life is a massive game changer. Yet, when things go wrong or we are disappointed in someone's behavior, we immediately resort to blame and criticism. Our thoughts revert to old thinking.

Remember when you were in school and the teacher asked the class, "Okay, who did it?" when something went wrong? If it were me, I wouldn't raise my hand right away. Who wanted to get punished? But, by not taking responsibility, we leave our thoughts open to suffering.

Complaining is the first sign that you have given up any responsibility for making the situation better. As soon as you start down this path, you come up with all the reasons why you are helpless.

You won't be able to be in a state of positivity if you are focused on building resentment or ill feelings toward other people. This doesn't mean that you must accept another person's behavior as okay. But you do have to take charge of your own attitude toward it.

People who take responsibility are in control of destiny. They are empowered by the choices they make. We can't control what is done to us, but we can take charge of our reaction toward it. You can interpret circumstances as events happening to you, but your decisions ultimately determine the outcome.

Building a positive mental mindset has to do with focusing on four specific areas of your life. By creating a healthy balance in each of these areas, you'll experience more peace of mind, harmony, and create more space in your mind for future success.

But the path to success begins with taking charge of your attitude and linking your thoughts to developing your attitude.

Now, write down your ideas for how you will take control of your attitude:

By doing at least three of these tasks every day, you'll develop a powerful mindset and empower your thoughts to become creative devices.

Here is a list of strategies you can try in developing your positive mental attitude.

Wake Up Early

Your brain is most active in the morning. Try getting up earlier than usual, reading for 20 minutes, or exercising. You can write a blog post or take your dog for an early walk. The time spent in the morning can be your most important time of the day because it sets the tone for your PMA throughout the rest of the day.

Meditate Twice a Day for 15 Minutes Each Session

Meditation clears your mind and enhances your concentration. By meditating, you gain greater control over your mental functions, and an increased ability to focus. It reduces your stress, improves your health, and reduces negative energy, while increasing your capacity to think up great ideas. Schedule in 15-minutes a day for meditation practice.

Learn Something New

A mind that is stagnant stays stuck in old beliefs and habits. Learning new skills and staying open to better ways of doing things frees your mind space up and makes room for more advanced learning. You could learn new skills to increase business opportunities or improve the quality of your relationships with friends and family.

By increasing your skills through committing to constant and never-ending improvement, you attract the people and situations that add greater value to life.

If Gandhi could take on the British Empire and practice forgiveness when surrounded by adversity, you can try to forgive one person and their defects. Write down the person's name. Then, write down three things they do well and praise them for it.

If you can't approach someone in person, you can write everything down and read it out loud. Visualize the person is there in the room with you. You will experience an amazing feeling of "letting go" with this activity.

Implementation: Write down three positive points about someone whom you struggle to get along with.

1.

2.

3.

Read Books on Personal Development

Try to schedule reading time every day and do it for at least 20 minutes. I spend upwards to an hour most days reading something. This has been a major contributor toward developing my positive attitude. Reading isn't just something you should do when you have time; it should be a part of your daily routine.

You can pencil in the time to read, instead of just doing it when you have time. This one daily habit of reading will set a positive tone for your mindset.

Here is a list of twenty life-changing books I recommend you add to your library of learning:

1. *The Miracle Morning* by **Hal Elrod**

2. *Awaken the Giant Within* by **Anthony Robbins**

3. *Eat That Frog* by **Brian Tracy**

4. *The Everyday Hero Manifesto by* **Robin Sharma**

5. *Antifragile by* **Nassim Nicholas Taleb**

6. *Can't Hurt Me* by **David Goggins**

7. *Atomic Habits* by **James Clear**

8. *The Obstacle is the Way* by **Ryan Holiday**

9. *The 7 Habits of Highly Effective People* by **Stephen R. Covey**

10. *The Success Principles: How to Get from Where You Are to Where You Want to Be* by **Jack Canfield**

11. *Greenlights* by **Matthew McConaughey**

12. *How to Win Friends and Influence People* by **Dale Carnegie**

13. *The High Five Habit by* **Mel Robbins**

14. *Principles by* **Ray Dalio**

15. *12 Rules for Life by* **Jordan B. Peterson**

16. *Will by* **Will Smith**

17. *Do the Hard Things First by* **Scott Allan**

18. *Mindset by* **Carol S. Dweck**

19. *Stop Doing That Sh*t by* **Gary John Bishop**

20. *The Greatest Salesman in the World by* **Og Mandino**

Now, add 10 more books you would like to put on your reading list. You can learn everything you have ever wanted by investing in a "$15-dollar mentor," or in other words, books that change lives.

Cheat Sheet: 25 Ways to Build Your Positive Mental Attitude

1. Ascertain what you most enjoy doing and do it as a labor of love with your heart and soul.

2. Understand that nobody can hurt your feelings, make you angry, or frighten you without your full cooperation and consent.

3. Don't cater to anyone who wants to exert a negative influence on you.

4. Break bad habits. Abstain from your vices one at a time, one per month, until you show yourself who the boss is.

5. Perceive that self-pity is an insidious destroyer of self-reliance. Believe that you are the one person upon whom you can and should depend at all times.

6. Relate to every circumstance in your life as something that has happened for the best.

7. Attune your mind to attract the things and situations you desire by expressing in a daily prayer your gratitude for what you already have.

8. Demand a reasonable number of dividends from life every day instead of waiting to receive them.

9. Live in a style that suits your physical and spiritual requirements.

10. Discern that personal power does not come from the possession of material things alone.

11. Exert yourself so that you keep your physical body in shape.

12. Reinforce the habit of tolerance.

13. Keep an open mind toward all people regardless of their differences, race, religion, or beliefs.

14. Learn to like people just as they are, instead of demanding that they be just as you want them to be.

15. Return every benefit that you receive with one of equal or greater value. This is the law of increasing returns.

16. Avoid the fear of old age by remembering nothing is ever taken from you without being replaced by something of equal or greater value.

17. Trust that adequate solutions can always be found, even if they are not the solutions you wanted or expected.

18. Remind yourself that any disadvantage can be overcome.

19. Welcome friendly criticism instead of reacting to it negatively; do not fear criticism but welcome it.

20. Embrace every opportunity to learn how others see you, and use it to take inventory of yourself and look for things that need improvement.

21. Create a mastermind alliance with others dedicated to the principles of success.

22. Grasp the differences between wishing and having a burning desire to achieve your goal. Burning desire gives you motivation, and it can be fueled by a positive attitude.

23. Abstain from negative conversations, especially complaining, gossip, or tearing apart another person's reputation. This conditions your mind to think negatively.

24. Discipline your mind to shape your destiny toward whatever purpose in life you have chosen.

25. Believe in the people you meet each and every day; they are doing their best just like you, even if their best doesn't match your standards.

Supercharge Your
Visual Imagination

"Your imagination is your preview of life's coming attractions." — Albert Einstein

One of the most powerful strategies for developing self-confidence and creating the life you want is mentally rehearsing the steps required to get you there. This is how concentrated visualization plays an important role in your success.

Having no vision for your life results in your lack of success, too.

When you can map out life's journey through your imagination, you are mentally rehearsing the actions needed to move straight to your goal. By focusing on your vision of how you want live, you attract the people and circumstances to help you get there.

Without a vision of what you want, you will always be at the mercy of circumstances created by others. But with your plan firmly in your mind, you can be confident that the road you're on is the right one.

Every success story begins with an idea, a vision, and a plan of action consisting of concrete steps to take you there.

The experiences you have are directly connected to the vision you create for yourself. A vision creates your new reality. You'll always hit your mark when you can see what you're aiming for. Start working on your vision right now. Set aside twenty minutes in the morning and evening for this exercise. Sit quietly and imagine the life you are leading.

Feed your imagination every day. Develop your vision of the life you want and pursue it relentlessly until it's yours. Don't stop thinking about it until it materializes. Focus, persist, and push your imagination to visualize the impossible.

One more vision you must consider. What will your life become if you don't achieve this thing? Will you live with the regret for the rest of your life? End up wasting your time and life doing work you hate? Always think "If only I had...." And spend the rest of your life with that question?

Think deeply about the consequences of not getting the life you want. You have this life right here and now. Make it count.

Remember that you are the captain of your own destiny, and you can Drive Your Destiny by taking charge of the vision you have to make it real.

Action Plan

Think about something you have always wanted to do. Is it a trip that you want to take, a change in jobs, or are you building your own online business? Do you visualize yourself becoming a successful entrepreneur? A published author? A researcher who discovers a new cure?

Now, choose the goal you feel most passionate about. Imagine the action steps you would need to take in order to reach this goal. How would you turn your vision into a reality? This is the stage where you mentally rehearse the steps you're taking to get to the inevitable outcome.

Now, imagine what happens if you don't get this. How will you feel? If you waste time and let this dream slip away, where do you see yourself?

> "I am enough of an artist to draw freely upon my imagination. Imagination is more important than knowledge. Knowledge is limited. Imagination encircles the world."
>
> — Albert Einstein

By tapping into the creativity of your unlimited imagination, the forces of the universe are triggered and immediately go to work to grant you all the things you can imagine, and much more. The things we create through the visual consciousness are those things we couldn't imagine for ourselves. The possibilities are endless.

Visualizing the life you intend to lead is setting up all future actions to pivot toward making it happen. You are not just visualizing what you want to achieve but how you are going to get there. It is about imagining the actions so that you know what to do.

Envisioning your day-to-day activities enables you to take intentional action when needed. By visualizing your success in anything, you create the framework for making it happen. When you envision yourself doing it, you eventually begin to do it.

How to Create Your Vision

Follow these steps:

1. First, know exactly what you want and what you have to do to get it.

   What do you really want?

2. When you see the object of your desire, hold it in your mind until it develops into a crystal-clear image of what it is you're going after.

   What does this "object" look like? Can you describe it in detail?

3. Feed your imagination every day. Develop your vision of the life you want and pursue it relentlessly until it's yours. Don't stop thinking about it until it materializes. Focus, persist, and push your imagination to the brink of mental exhaustion.

Do you have a time of day you block in for this activity? What images appear as you visualize your destiny?

4. Think positive thoughts and utilize clear, intense emotion. Be passionate about your vision, and you will develop the ability to manifest what you desire.

When you sit in silence and visualize the life you desire, what are your thoughts?

5. Believe in your vision. You must have complete faith in the visual imagination of your dreams. Erase all doubt and use affirmations to build a foundation of faith and positive energy. People who doubt the power they have within eventually fail to produce the results they want. Your belief is the fuel to making it happen!

What is your affirmation or motivational script for manifesting this desire?

Action Plan: Visualize Your Future in the Now

1. Visualize your life ten years from now. Visualize the person you are. What areas of your life must you focus on to move you from here to there.

What if: It is your birthday and your closest friends and family are celebrating with you. Someone whose life you helped to change is giving a speech about you. What are they saying?

2. Think about something you have always wanted to do. Is it a trip that you want to take, a change in jobs, or are you building your own online business? Do you visualize yourself becoming a successful entrepreneur? A published author? A researcher who discovers a new cure?

    Write down your ideas in your journal.

3. Now, choose the goal you feel most passionate about. Imagine the action steps you would need to take in order to reach this goal. How would you turn your vision into a reality? This is the stage where you mentally rehearse the steps you're taking to get to the inevitable outcome.

By doing this exercise, you can effectively walk through the steps before a single action is taken. You are setting up your mind to move forward and take action.

Answer these questions in your journal, or use the space below:

- What would you do if there were no limitations to the kind of life you desire?
- How would you spend the rest of your days if you could do absolutely anything with your time?
- What would it take for you accomplish everything you have ever dreamed possible?
- What would make you the happiest person alive?
- What are the opportunities available to you right now?

- What is stopping you from taking advantage of these opportunities?
- What opportunities do you wish you had? How will you create these opportunities?
- What event do you envision that will have a profound impact on your life?
- What earth-changing events do you visualize taking place in the world in the next fifty years?

- What is the life you visualize living someday?

- What actions could you take every day to bring you closer to achieving this dream?

Let your imagination run wild with all the things you have always imagined doing. Let go of the idea that you have to be realistic about what is possible; this is where our limitations exist.

Remember that people who live in fear of existing outside their comfort zone are limiting themselves. If you want a life that makes a difference, you have to live differently.

Become unconventional in your thinking. You have to "be" who you want to become. You have to run through the mental process while taking confident action to move closer to your goal.

The source of your greatest power is not something you have to obtain. It isn't something you have to work for or earn: it's yours! You already have all the tools you need.

What you have been lacking is not knowledge or skill but a vision for the life you want to be leading.

By training your mind to see what success looks like, it starts to put the pieces into place. You notice the actions you need to take, and then self-doubt and uncertainty slip away. You erase the pathways that once focused on constant failure.

> "The universe is change; our life is what our thoughts make it."
>
> — Marcus Aurelius

However, simply visualizing the life you want isn't enough. You need to take your deepest passions and put them into action by building solid intentions around everything you want to create.

In order to do this, you can:

- Use visual meditation for twenty minutes each morning. Visualize the exact reality you want to experience in the future.

- Repeat positive affirmations at the start of each day and again when the day is winding down.

- Create a master goal for your life. Spend twenty to thirty minutes each day imagining the success of this goal. See it in your mind's eye as having already been achieved.

- Play inspirational music to keep you inspired and motivated. As you listen to the music, visualize the activities you are performing that take you closer to fulfilling your vision.

- Practice optimum visualization technique to accomplish amazing results! Plan at least three sessions a week.

- Start a visionary journal or blog and record your thoughts and visions on paper. This enhances your experience of the creative visualization process.

- Create a visual storyboard. You can draw, paint or use pictures to create a collage of your vision.

Supercharge Your
Self-Compassion

"Owning our story and loving ourselves through that process is the bravest thing that we'll ever do."

— Brene Brown

Many of our struggles branch out from our ability to structuralize the experiences attached to mistakes, failures, and disappointment in ourselves. Being kind to yourself could be an experience you are not familiar with. Your mind could still be stuck on the pains of your past and blaming someone —your parents, an old relationship, or former boss—for your failures and shortcomings in life.

The solutions is to develop a deeper sense of self-love and compassion, not only in your relationships but, the relationship with yourself. YOU are the most important person in the universe!

I know, we are taught to think otherwise because this is perceived as an egotistical approach. But if you don't care for yourself, you will fail to care for others. Instead of getting your love 100%, they are receiving 20%. The rest is lost in self-loathing, worry, regret and the internal war of negative emotions you carry with you.

Right now, I want you to write down a few words that express how you really feel about you. Make a list of 10 traits or characteristics that you love about yourself. If this is too difficult right now, bookmark this and come back to it later. But please do it!

For example:

- I help people when they need money

- I show people the way to make life better.

- I'm a great listener.

- I'm kind, generous and care for the well-being of people.

The path to successful living is through gratitude, compassion and self-love—for yourself and other fellows. The "soul" purpose of this journey isn't about becoming successful but, learning to live successfully. In order to do this, self-compassion plays a critical role.

Imagine what you could accomplish, where you could go, and who you could become if you had a level of compassion for yourself so deep that nothing could break it.

When you love who you are at the highest level, you will never fear the future or hold onto resentment and regrets in the past. You will form the thoughts of forgiveness, not for the mistakes you've made in the past, but you will practice the art of forgiving yourself for these mistakes.

When you love and let go of this fear, you invite the gift of compassion into your life.

Self-compassion ties everything together. When you can embrace that deeper love for who you are, your mission, and the importance you bring to this world, compassion begins with clarity of your mindful intent.

If failing has always been your fear, the solution to breaking this fear is self-kindness. You are on this path to fail with happiness. To fail knowing you are cared for. To fail knowing there is no failure, but lessons learned on a never-ending journey of continuous growth and self-improvement.

> "When you say 'Yes' to others, make sure you are not saying 'No' to yourself."
>
> — Paulo Cohelo

Self-Compassion is an Act of Surrender

One of the difficulties in giving into self-compassion is giving up the trap of childhood fears and securities. There are memories, emotions and attachments that keep you glued to your past because that is a place of comfortability, even if it hurts to stay there.

Do you experience moments when you're trapped in the past and are unable to break free? I know I do. It gets very intense and I begin to spiral down as if all hope for the future is melting away. This isn't a healthy way to live, but the experience can be very real when going through it.

The trigger is your thoughts. You latch onto an experience from the past when you failed, made a decision you later regret, or a situation that didn't turn out as you had hoped for.

If there is a decision or event from your past that you're holding onto, make a note of it here:

When this happens, I surrender to the experience and let the thoughts pass through my mind. Like water, you can let it flow through you. Thoughts have a way of making everything appear real, as if it's happening right now. The mind doesn't know the difference between what is happening in real time or what your imagination is conjuring up.

But in these times, remember: You control your thoughts. You're creating them. You can also change and shift your thoughts as easily as moving a stick shift from neutral to drive.

Write down you're answer to these questions:

- Do you believe you are responsible for your own self-care?

- Do you like and accept yourself even when rejected by others?

- Do you love and support yourself even when others don't?

- Do you feel good about yourself most of the time? Some of the time? Not at all? (There are no right answers, just answer the best you can).

- Are you worthy of loving yourself 100% without validation? (Hint: The answer is YES, I AM!)

If you're looking for validation that you're okay, how about this: you made it. You're here. You can now look yourself in the mirror and say, "Here I am. I did it!" You have survived this journey and now you can thrive for the rest of it

Be certain your thoughts and actions are guiding you in the right direction. Surrender to the faith that you are on a journey of incredible circumstances and that, not everyone gets this chance. You have been handed a gift, and now you have to open it to see what is inside.

The greatest gift anyone can receive is from the heart, and as you heal from the patterns of your past, push self-defeat aside to make space for new relationships, and a new way of living that only failing big can bring you. This is the essence of surrendering to a bigger vision for yourself.

Everyone is broken to some extent, but that is where your strength can be found. I like what Ernest Hemmingway said: "The world breaks everyone, and afterward, some are strong at the broken places."

As we learn to accept ourselves as human beings on a spiritual journey, it becomes a simpler process of self-acceptance. You are not meant to be perfect in all the things you do, but the perfection is doing these things with failed intention.

You may try and not succeed, but you keep trying, and without fail, you will move past the broken patterns of denial and self-delusion.

Tara Brach, the author of Radical Acceptance, has said:

"Feeling compassion for ourselves in no way releases us from responsibility for our actions. Rather, it releases us from the self-hatred that prevents us from responding to our life with clarity and balance."

I created a powerful affirmation that I use every morning. I read it to myself out loud at the start of each day. It sets the course for the day and aligns all thoughts with my positive mental attitude.

You can write out your personal affirmation here (Refer to the chapter on creating your vision statement):

Life is Flawed, Fragile and Filled with Suffering

Self-compassion is grounded in holding yourself responsible. You can no longer blame or hold a grudge against the people who wronged or hurt you. It is the buildup of this resentment that destroys your peace of mind.

If you want to be unkind to yourself, walk around with hate in your heart and mind. It is a terrible form of mental illness that you create for yourself. Remember, you are always in control of the madness that fills your mind.

The next time you are feeding into your victim mentality, you can stop yourself and flip it around. Refuse to go there. Refuse to be the victim anymore. This is self-empowerment. This is you taking a stand and saying NO to the negative emotions that rise up to destroy you.

Now you have the tools and the know-how. You have the courage and the wisdom. You have the answers, and sometimes you don't have the answers, and it's okay to admit this. What matters is that you end the verbal and mental abuse targeted towards the one person you should love the most...yourself.

Failing to love and accept yourself sets you up for failing in other areas where self-care is a priority. If you fail to care for YOU, it is difficult to express this true compassion for anyone else.

Love begins with self-compassion, and like a spider's web, it branches out to everyone from there. People will be attracted to you because you radiate this from within.

"When you begin to touch your heart or let your heart be touched, you begin to discover that it's bottomless, that it doesn't have any resolution, that this heart is huge, vast, and limitless. You begin to

discover how much warmth and gentleness is there,
as well as how much space."

— PEMA CHÖDRÖN, author of
Welcoming the Unwelcome

As the Buddhists have been teaching for centuries, compassion begins with the self. It's from this place of self-compassion that genuine love extends into the mind and heart. It is fully recognizing your human journey and the gifts you carry with you to share with the world.

Here are two exercises to building a deeper relationship with yourself and others. You can focus on performing one exercise every week.

When you feel yourself moving into that deeper place of self-compassion, try another activity. These practices are a mix of meditation, mindfulness, and breathing. You are now going to focus on what Kristin Neff calls "Ending the madness".

Shift Your Critical Self-Talk

There is a monster inside of you, and it tears you apart with every chance it gets. This critical monster has grown very strong over the years, and as you may have noticed, it is difficult to control.

This is your internal critic that unleashes rants of demoralizing words and it appears to happen so naturally, you rarely notice it when it is taking place. But when you mess up or fail big time, it's there to remind you of your failure.

It sounds like this:

- "Now you've gone and done it!"

- "Now look at this. You think you're going to succeed if you can't do this one simple thing?"

The first step to turning down your internal noise is awareness that it's there. Just acknowledge its presence when it begins throwing insults at you.

Being critical of others is just as harmful as the critic that beats you up. Either way it goes, the voice is a negative force that has a sole purpose to destroy your confidence and compassion.

Focus on your awareness of self-criticism.

One practice is to soften this voice. Treat your negative voices with compassion. Don't talk back or get angry. This inner voice is still you, it is just the uglier, angrier version of you. It can be talked down with gentle persuasion and compassion. It is the child or young adult that is on the fence, ready to defend.

Directed criticism

When feeling inadequate, you go on the attack and look for the "worst traits" in people. This leads to judgment and tearing apart another person's reputation.

When this happens, how will you stop it?

The Seven-Day Anti-Criticism Challenge

Criticism is a destructive form of negativity. Delivered in the wrong pitch or manner, it can destroy someone's confidence and leave them emotionally "crippled" for life. If you grew up in an environment that weighed heavily on criticism to succeed, you know the damage that this can cause. I recommend you take the Seven-Day Anti-Criticism Challenge.

Make a challenge with yourself that you are not going to criticize or say anything negative about anyone, no matter what they do. This does not mean you have to be passive and just accept everything they do. Seek another way to express your feelings that is not along the lines of criticism or judgment.

Try this for seven days. You will fail at this if self-criticism or directed criticism is a habit. When you fail, make note of the date and time. Start again right away. Start with a new slate. Don't wait for the next day to roll around.

Once I stopped, everything changed — my perspective, my mood, and my desire to be right. It also eliminated my need to counterattack, which was one of my core negative coping strategies.

For the next seven days, you are going to make a promise to yourself not to criticize or condemn yourself or others in any way. This will require a great amount of self-discipline. And you will likely fail many times. But that is okay. The goal is to eliminate your need to criticize yourself or others.

Once you hit the 7-day mark, your next challenge is to hit 14 days. Imagine your level of compassion for yourself and other human beings when you hit this mark.

I recommend using a calendar to mark off every day you succeeded without having a critical thought about yourself or another person. By marking it down on a calendar, you can see the progress you are making.

The 2-Way Mirror Strategy

This is a great technique for calming anxiety and lowering your nervousness so that you can become comfortable just being yourself. Spend a few minutes with yourself in front of a mirror. It may feel uncomfortable at first, but after a few days, it will become your favorite habit. Do this for just a few minutes in the morning. To save time, do it while styling your hair, shaving, putting on makeup, or brushing your teeth.

Talk positively to yourself. Do not criticize or condemn anything about yourself. Talk to yourself as if you were talking to a best friend. Be the best friend you have ever had. Give yourself positive advice.

Write down the affirmations or positivity quotes you will use:

Look yourself in the eye and just give yourself advice as if you would give it to someone you care about. Do this technique for ten minutes a day, first thing in the morning. It builds your confidence, centers your thoughts, and enhances self-compassion.

Here are a few prompts:

- Talk about an achievement you recently had. Praise yourself and give credit for something you recently did.
- Talk about the great day you are going to have. Pump yourself up by talking about all the great things you are going to do today. Will you spend time with friends, family, or your children? Will you do something fun that you have been looking forward to? The purpose of this is to get yourself into a positive frame of mind and to develop a healthy mindset for the day.
- Talk about someone you love and admire. This is a great way to start feeling good about people again. Talk to yourself about the most important people in your life.
- Talk about someone you have resentment toward. Just as it is important to talk about the people you love; now talk about someone you have a difficult

relationship with. Think of one good thing you can say about this person.

Imagine he or she is staring back at you as you are having a conversation. This strategy removes the negative energy that builds up when you have to deal with difficult people.

The Substitution Technique for Lasting Change

In order to generate a mindful mind and bring your compassion to the surface, you can apply the substitution technique to reinforce positive self-talk.

It works like this:

If you are in the habit of talking down (self-criticizing) about yourself, you can turn this around using this replacement technique. Instead of talking negatively to yourself with "I suck at this", you could say, "I am now learning how to do this better."

The objective is to reinforce your thoughts with positive anecdotes and words that support you. Begin by replacing the negative thoughts you have with empowering thoughts. Substitute your default belief that you're no good with a belief that empowers you.

Do not accept any thought that builds on your doubt and fear. Instead of "I am no good", you say, "I am great"; "My life sucks" is substituted with "I am grateful to have everything that I do." You can make a list of your gratitude and refer to this list when doing this activity.

Now, use the substitution technique for replacing:

- Harmful, negative words with positive expressions. You can include affirmations that work amazingly well when it comes to forming a positive mindset.

- Worry-based, fearful thinking with positive images that encourage immediate action. This will move you closer toward your objectives.

- Destructive bad habits with good habits that lead to positive results while creating a better process for doing things.

The Substitution Technique in Action

When you catch yourself criticizing either yourself or others, you can replace this behavior with the opposite action. Instead of criticizing and judging, speak well of others. Build up their reputation. Stop yourself immediately and change this behavior from condemning and verbal criticism to praising the reputation of others.

Challenge yourself to do this for one week. Make it a conscious habit to convert all negative actions, behaviors, and conversations into a stream of positive conviction.

Tell yourself, "I am so happy you're here."

Tell others, "You are great! I am so happy to have you in my life!"

Self-compassion and compassion towards others are a powerful gift. I want you to embrace this gift and make it a part of you. This isn't a random act of kindness but something to practice every minute of the day. When you find your compassion slipping away and need to reconnect, meditation and practicing mindfulness will bring you back to the center.

The journey toward self-love is a balance of doing things for yourself, and what is expected of you. But what matters isn't what the world expects but what you expect from yourself.

Only you can make yourself happy. I know this sound like arbitrary common sense or old-style advice, but have you ever placed your dependence for love on someone else and ended up disappointed? Exactly. Nobody can provide you 24/7 with that feeling of self-compassion. Nobody can feed you the thoughts that go into creating your positive mindset.

You are the master gardener of your mind, body, and spirit. So, live that way. Do nice things for yourself. Treat your life as if it is a great creation. Do this and you'll always be working on the self-love model.

Final suggestions:

Open Honesty

You should be completely honest with yourself. Stay true to what you know is right. Accept it when you are feeling fearful and uncertain. This is a sign that you could be slipping back into an old routine. Accept yourself with all your flaws and don't criticize yourself or others for theirs. People will make mistakes and screw things up. That's what we do.

Practice Self-Acceptance

It is hard for many of us to like ourselves as we are. As we truly are, right now, without having an attachment to the past or the future. This is the area in which we fight to balance our lives.

Let's take the past as an example. We have all been through experiences and made mistakes. We have hurt others and we have been hurt. Many hold on to regret and pain from childhood that has morphed over time into a deeper form of negativity that transforms into depression, anger, or rage. The bottom line is, our past selves cannot be corrected, only accepted.

20-minute thought meditation

This has proven to be a very powerful calming exercise. You probably have some idea how it works so I'll just run through the meditation exercise steps again.

1. Play a piece of relaxing music.

2. You can sit in a chair or in a relaxed position.

3. Breathe in and out deeply. Breathe in deeply, and exhale for five seconds.

4. Focus on your thoughts and try to keep them still. You could also run positive affirmations through your mind.

5. Make this a consistent habit you can tap into on a regular basis.

Visit your "past" child

Imagine that you could go back in time to visit yourself when you were a kid. Choose a painful memory that you are holding onto. Approach the child version of yourself and embrace him or her. Hold them for as long as you can. Tell them you love them.

If you think this exercise sounds silly and your response is, "No way am I doing that," that's okay, but try it just once. It really is an amazing exercise that works if you keep doing it. You will connect with the biggest part of who you were.

Make a note of how you feel about this experience.

Taking care of your health

It amazes me how I see people damaging themselves physically. Eating poorly, smoking, drinking in excess, or overworking. We put ourselves through a lot of pain that isn't reflective of someone who loves themselves. This is the pain point of addictions or activities that damage us.

When we fail to take care of our bodies, we are essentially limiting the long life we could have. Don't you want to live as long as you can? If you were on your deathbed now, wouldn't you long for more time with your children or loved ones? Think about that. If this was your last day on earth, how would you spend it?

Don't end it with regret. If you have some habits that need to be controlled and changed in order to live a healthier lifestyle, then become aware of what they are. Create a vision of yourself who's feeling good because you are looking after yourself.

Change the way you eat. Stop eating anything that is shaving years off your life. How you treat your body in terms of exercise, eating habits, and addictions is a direct reflection of how you are valuing the life you have.

If you don't value your life, you don't love yourself enough. If you are eating badly and taking substances that have long-term damaging effects, you won't enjoy quality of life.

Spend time doing things you truly enjoy

If you're struggling with shame, enjoying pleasurable activities can be seen as something you don't deserve. But each and every one of us deserves to engage in joyful, uplifting, and exciting experiences.

Allowing yourself to experience true happiness—to take time from your life to do something you love—is an act of compassion.

When I found myself feeling ashamed for a mistake I'd made, I began making a conscious effort to understand what situation provoked that act and I strove to make choices that put me in more positive situations.

Forgiving Past Mistakes

Forgiveness is vital for self-compassion. We all make mistakes, but not all of us forgive ourselves for them. Depending on the mistake, this can be a very daunting task, but keep in mind that you cannot go back (no matter how badly you might want to), so the best thing to do is to choose forgiveness and forward motion.

Whenever I did something inappropriate, instead of shrugging it off or excusing my behavior, I started apologizing for it, both to others and to myself. Again, I focused on the fact that I wasn't bad; it was my behavior that was.

Rewire your mindset

Sadly, it's often challenging to lift yourself up (particularly if you're feeling really low or ashamed), but if you want to create compassion for yourself, you have to change your mindset.

For me, self-compassion started with changing my thoughts. I started focusing on the fact that my behavior was bad, not me. Once I started labeling behavior (instead of myself as whole), I was able to be kinder to myself and open up my mind to the possibility that I could make changes.

Practice Your Self-Compassion Affirmations

Here are ten self-compassion affirmations I use. You can create your own in the notes below:

1. I accept the best and worst aspects of who I am.

2. Changing is never simple but it's easier if I stop being hard on myself.

3. My mistakes just show that I'm growing and learning.

4. It's okay to make mistakes and forgive myself.

5. I am free to let go of others' judgments.

6. It's safe for me to show kindness to myself.

7. I deserve compassion, tenderness, and empathy from myself.

8. I release myself with forgiveness from today and move forward with self-love to tomorrow.

9. Every day is a new opportunity. I won't let self-doubt or judgment hold me back from the future.

10. I forgive myself and accept my flaws because nobody is perfect.

11. I'm not the first person to have felt this way, and I won't be the last, but I'm growing.

Self-Kindness: A Letter to Yourself

Write to yourself as you would to someone you care deeply about. Having reminded yourself that you're not perfect or immune from painful feelings, this is the space to be comforting.

Building a Positive Self-Image

First of all, let me ask you these questions. Take your time to think about them if needed. Your answers will help to clarify the best path to take when it comes to building and creating your positive self-image.

Questions for thought:

1. What are you feeling about yourself right now?

2. If someone asked you, "Are you successful?" what would you say?

3. If someone asked you, "Are you a failure?" what would you say?

4. If someone asked you to define yourself in twenty words or less, how would you respond?

5. After reading through the four negative mindsets, what mindset impacts you the most? How has this affected your positive self-image?

6. Who are you blaming for the negative experiences in your life? Are you ready to let this go?

You can write out your answers on the notes sheet at the end of this section.

The "Not Now" Technique

One technique I employed over the years is what I call the "not now" technique. Whenever my mind began racing with fearful, negative thoughts that switched on those voices feeding into my head, I would simply say, "not now" and turn it off.

By inserting these words, I was interrupting the flow of negativity. In doing this, I made myself aware of what was happening instead of just letting it happen. I was free to choose the thoughts I wanted, and create the language that communicates with my mind.

What thoughts did you turn off today? How will you use this strategy tomorrow?

The Formula for Empowering Your Image

It takes time to build up an empowering and confident image of yourself. As we set out to make changes in our emotional and mental states, we find that we are up against those inner voices that won't leave us alone. They are not real. They are simply impressions of old voices and opinions that your mind has recorded. But that doesn't mean they hurt any less. We can control these voices so that they stay silent. After all, you are in total control of your own mind.

Up until now it just appeared that you had no choice in how you were living. But we know that isn't true. You can empower your character to no limits.

How to Overcome Negative Conditioning

It is easy for us to judge others because they can't fight back. But do you consider how the world sees you? Take this a step further. How do you visualize yourself? Are you a positive influence?

For many years, I wasn't. I had a bad habit of seeing the worst in others and using that as a benchmark to sum up their character. But seeing the damaging effect that it had on my emotional well-being, I made a concrete decision not to be that type of person.

We should set boundaries within ourselves. For example, can you catch yourself when you start to criticize your mistakes or when you fail to meet your goals or personal expectations? Do you have healthy boundaries that kick in when you have gone too far in undermining yourself and comparing yourself to other people?

It is one thing when boundaries are elicited upon us. We are expected to follow rules, and many of us do, but how about the rules we set for ourselves?

Draw the line on your negative patterns of defeat. By drawing on your self-actualization, you can consciously choose what is acceptable. You don't have to wait for permission.

Make a note of how you see yourself as a positive influence in the world around you:

Practice self-compassion 24/7

Be good to yourself by engaging in fulfilling activities that add to self-esteem and self-love. Here are some examples:

- Get plenty of rest.

- Spend time with someone talking about the journey you are both taking.

- Think about the many things you're grateful for in life.

- Stop trying to overachieve. Focus on self-development as your primary goal.

In addition to the above suggestions, I recommend that you have frequent review sessions with yourself. Take a look at the areas of your life that need the most work.

Is it in your relationships with people?

Are you physically out of shape?

Do you suffer from negativity that keeps invading your thoughts?

Whatever it is, come up with several action steps you can implement to overcome the obstacle. For example, maybe you've been treating your body badly for many years by smoking, eating junk food, or drinking too much.

In order to reach that level of fulfillment in which you are happy with your physical self, you could get help to put an end to any addictive behavior you have. If you are overweight, you can start by eating better or joining a weight loss program.

Self-compassion involves tough self-love. You have to look at who you want to be, who you are now, and identify with what you don't like about yourself. We can only become the person we truly want to be by recognizing the person we are and the traits or habits that are damaging to us.

I suggest the following actions:

- Set up weekly sessions to review where you are.

- Identify the people you can reach out to for help.

- Do at least one activity a week that you enjoy, which brings you fulfillment.

- Stay resilient on the path that is committed to your continuous growth.

Supercharge Your
Best Habits

"Feeling sorry for yourself, and your present condition is not only a waste of energy but the worst habit you could possibly have."

— Dale Carnegie

Your habits can make or break you. More people fail because of their bad habits than from anything else. Sometimes all it takes is breaking one bad habit, and you can change your behavior and way of living for the better.

How can you break the bad habits that are failing you, interrupt the pattern, and turn your fails into wins?

Some of these bad habits might include:

- Watching TV in excess

- Smoking

- Browsing the Internet with your smartphone

- Eating junk food

- Staying up too late

- Not drinking enough water

- Procrastination

- Playing video games for three hours a day

- Impulse shopping

Bad habits are draining, but a system of good habits supported by a disciplined routine can defeat the habits holding you back. Many of us have been living with our old habits for so long that we don't recognize them as the reason behind internal failure.

Break Bad Habits: The 7-Step Approach:

1. Identify the specific problem the bad habit is causing you.

2. Identify the habit you want to stop.

3. Create an action plan for the next 30 days.

4. Review your progress after 30 days.

5. Reset the clock for another 30 days.

6. Be aware of your triggers.

7. Focus on long-term change.

We need long-term focus and consistent concentration over a two-month period to make change happen. If you are expecting to see massive gains after two weeks, you could be setting yourself up to fail. Think long-term habit change and stay focused on daily repetitions.

Your habits are life-changing actions repeated again and again every day. Focus on one habit change at a time.

When you are comfortable that the habit has become a regular part of your thinking, try changing another one.

Action Prompt: Eliminate Bad Habits!

- Make a list of the habits you want to change.

- Next to each habit, write down the reason why you want to change it.

- Create a list of new action steps to change it. Instead of watching TV for 4 hours, what will you do? Instead of eating junk food every night before bed, what can you eat that is healthy?

- Focus on changing one habit for the next 60 days. After you're confident the habit has taken hold, move onto the next one.

Supercharge Your Habit Program

1. Visualize living the new habit

A new habit can be hard to instill in yourself but imagine how it will change your life. How would you look and feel after three months of steady exercise? Where would your career be if you dedicated thirty minutes a day to reading books on building a business?

How would you change mentally and emotionally if you were meditating for ten minutes every day?

In the first part of this book, we discussed visual imagination. You can use this tactic for forming new habits. Say you want to lose weight, but you have a habit of eating junk food every night. You can visualize what you'll look like after dropping twenty pounds. You can visualize the habit of exercising in the evening instead of just watching TV and consuming junk. In doing so, you will create the emotions that go with it.

2. Focus on the daily action, and not the end goal

It is easy to focus on the end goal. But it doesn't stop there. If you form the habit of eating less junk food and more greens so that you can lose thirty pounds, what happens when you reach your goal? You mind could trick you into thinking, "This is it," and revert back to your old routine again.

Keep setting new goals for yourself so that you're always improving. Stay fixed on what you can achieve each day. Be realistic, as well. Instead of deciding you'll lose twenty pounds, stay focused on not eating junk food for today, or doing twenty minutes of cardio exercise.

3. Focus on one habit at a time

There are dozens of habits we could try to change next week. Habits we want to break, and habits we want to start. I would recommend focusing on one new habit until it is fixed. Then you can scale up and start another one.

Can you imagine where you would be in six months if you committed to just one course of action? Focusing on one habit can have a tremendous impact. If you try to change several habits at once, you'll become frustrated when you start to miss a day here and there, and then one failure becomes many. One habit is a manageable goal.

4. Create an action plan for each habit and repeat

The goal is to commit to a set action plan for each day. This can be as simple as committing to five minutes per day doing a single action. For example, if you're trying to build the exercise habit, you can do just five reps on the first day. If you are writing a book, commit to writing for ten minutes for the next thirty days.

What matters isn't how much we get done. The idea is to follow through with the action and make it a consistent pattern you perform everyday, regardless if it is ten reps or fifty. You can scale up later when you are conditioned to doing the action without thinking about it.

5. Repeat this action every day for the next thirty days

You can commit to the same time each day, which is the best situation. For example, write two hundred words of your novel first thing in the morning at six a.m.

Meditate for ten minutes every evening an hour before bed.

If you think about it, you already perform hundreds of habits a day unconsciously at roughly the same time each day. Now, we're making ourselves aware of the new habit by pushing it into our schedule and making it a regular occurrence.

6. Be realistic in your expectations

Change takes time. We have to be patient with our progress and resilient in our approach. The people who become masters at what they do reach that level through decades of practice. Tony Robbins said, "We overestimate what we can do in a month but underestimate our progress in a year."

If you have had the same habit for years, it is deeply ingrained into your mind. Expecting to replace your habit with a new one takes time, and it could take up to six months. Even then, you have to continue practicing the new habit.

7. Keep it simple

Habit building isn't complicated. You can keep it simple by trying the following:

- Focus on one habit a time.
- Perform the same action every day.
- And at the same time every day.
- Scale up gradually.

- Measure your results.

8. Create your habit triggers

Set up a trigger for your new habit. This works for both creating new ones and breaking your bad habits. For example, if your new habit is to read for ten minutes a day, leave the book you are reading on the table in the morning so that it's the first thing you see.

Whatever your focus is for building this habit, you can leave it out in the morning, or set an alarm to go off at a certain time each day. For example, I scheduled my habit time in my calendar. That way I would receive a notification when it was time to take action.

The trigger becomes your permission to take action. Make it visible. Make it so loud that you can't ignore it.

9. Be aware of bad habit triggers

Just as we need triggers to take action toward positive habits, we also need to be aware of the triggers that pull us back into bad habits. For example, when I reduced the amount of junk food I was eating, I had a habit of trolling through the junk food aisle in the store. As soon as I walked into the store it was the first section I visited. Then, if they were having a sale on chocolate that day, my trigger would associate cheap chocolate with pleasure, and I would give in.

Whatever habit you're working on replacing, make yourself aware of the habits that trigger you to give in and eat, spend, or indulge. The danger lies in our own minds. It is your thinking that causes you to seek out the trigger spot. You might be working on replacing smoking with exercise, and then after a workout, you stroll by a cigar shop because it's on your way home.

In the early stages of habit changing, we are vulnerable to our cravings and what a mentor of mine called "crooked thinking." Make yourself aware of the habits that draw you into relapsing.

People relapse all the time, in many cases because the old habit returns when they don't get results after a week or two. We then unconsciously seek out our old routines because they are familiar. New habits have a certain level of discomfort until they become solidified.

If you relapse, try again. The key is to focus on daily positive action.

10. Set manageable goals

Let's say our decision is to create a habit for reading more books. This would increase your knowledge and would be a better activity than watching TV. If you stick with thirty minutes of reading per day, you could read five books in a month. But if thirty minutes is a tough habit to stick with, try just ten minutes a day. This is easily manageable.

In fact, most habits could be built in just five to ten minutes per day. You don't have to invest an hour every day or push yourself to the end of exhaustion.

Break it down into small chunks and you'll have created your new habit within thirty days. You want to write a book? Start with one hundred words per day. You want to wake up earlier? Start by setting your alarm ten minutes earlier. You could also build a habit to go to bed earlier. Remember it's not the big result that we're going for, but building the behavior. Once you master the routine, you can scale up at any time.

11. Focus on long-term conversion

It takes time to change behaviors. If it happened quickly, everyone would be doing it. According to a study released in the European Study of Social Psychology, a team of researchers led by Phillippa Lally surveyed ninety-six people over twelve weeks to find out how long it took them to develop a new habit. At the end of the survey, Lally analyzed the results of the experiment and determined the time it took to form a new habit was approximately sixty-six days.

We need to think long-term. It takes approximately sixty-six days to replace a habit. This is a tough road to navigate for most people.

We need long-term focus and consistent concentration over a period of months to make it happen. If you are expecting to see massive gains after two weeks, you could be setting yourself up to fail. Think long-term habit change, and stay focused on daily repetitions.

An example would be pushups. I do fifty to seventy-five pushups four times per week. But it took me nearly three months to build up to this. I started by doing five a day for the first week, then ten a day in the second week. Then I increased by two push-ups a day until I hit my goal of fifty a day. Every day, I would add two more to the habit. By focusing on the long-term objective, which was to build up to one hundred a day, I could achieve this and get into better shape than ever before.

Action Plan:

Have a long-term focus and scale up slowly. Whatever your habit, you can achieve your goal by scaling slowly. Stay fixed on the behavior.

12. Focus on habit replacement instead of elimination

When it comes to building new habits, our initial thought is, "I have to eliminate the old habits." If you want to eat healthier to lose weight and get into better shape, eliminating junk food intake isn't a realistic plan. Instead, focus on reducing the habit a little bit every week.

Reduce your sugar intake every day by ten percent. You'll have less pressure to do it perfectly. You can apply this to any habit you are attempting to break. Want to reduce the amount of time you spend online? Start cutting down by five percent a day. You can set up blocks of time when you're offline altogether instead of wired to your cellphone or computer.

To get away from constantly looking at your cell phone, consider buying a regular alarm clock and a watch. This will prevent you from using your phone as an alarm, and keep you from looking at it as soon as you wake up. Now that you have a watch, you won't need to check your phone for the time—which means you won't get distracted by other notifications on your screen, either.

Action Plan:

Reduce your habits by five percent a day. Don't simply eliminate. Then you can hit your goals much more realistically. Focus on reduction, not elimination.

13. Build support through accountability

New habits are difficult to implement and stick with, especially in the beginning. For this reason, having a habit buddy is a recommended approach to supporting your new routine.

If you're trying to get into the habit of exercising more, this could be someone you go jogging with twice a week, or you might do strength training together. If you can't meet in person, you can connect via Zoom, Skype, or Google Hangouts.

Set up a habit accountability call with your friend once a week to follow up on progress. Make sure you work with someone who is also interested in habit development, although they could be working on a different habit. It's important to share not just the fun of habit building, but the struggles you are going through as well.

Action Plan:

Find a habit support buddy. Connect once per week—online, on the phone, or in person—to discuss your progress or any difficulties you've experienced.

14. Throw out the all or nothing approach

If you've had a slip, get back into it. We all miss a day in our routine. What matters is that you can pick it up again the next day. If you let it go too long, you risk starting over again. If that happens, and it probably could, begin again. The only time you fail is if you give up and revert back to your old habit.

Let yourself make mistakes along the way and learn what works and what doesn't. Changing a habit is about consistency. It's not about how much or how many, but how often. This is the frequency with which you take action.

If we expect perfection, we can also expect to fail. An all or nothing mindset often stops people from setting up new behaviors. I don't know of anyone who has a perfect track record.

Habits take time and persistence, but most of all, patience. We have to be ready to forgive ourselves again and again. I have broken several bad habits this way, but in some cases, it took years.

Habits are the thick strands of success built upon daily patterns of consistent practice and repetition of proven successful actions. These patterns make up the daily routines that mold an unbreakable cycle of conditioning.

It is the consistent repetition of these key behaviors that builds the foundation for your life—the same patterns repeated over and over again, programming you for success, failure, or a mediocre existence.

You are the master programmer and architect of your own life. Habits are the tools you should master if you are to build the foundations of a good life.

Supercharge Your
Personal Growth

"The swiftest way to triple your success is to double your investment in personal development."

— Robin Sharma

One of the core foundations in living an extraordinary life is the commitment and effort you put into personal growth. To be successful, to grow and learn so as to be the best version of yourself requires a consistent commitment to the learning curve for scaling up your skill set.

You always must be working to become better, learn more, and apply what you have learned. Your personal growth never ends. There is no deadline or age limit. But I've seen many people who reached a plateau or level of status in their lives and made the conscious decision they had done enough.

Personal growth is the foundation of success. It is a commitment to continuously improve your life in the areas of mindset, spirituality, financial, intellectual, emotional, and physical health.

Your life is an ongoing process of experience and learning. When you quit a job, or move to a new location, you have to start over again and learn a new skill, acquire more knowledge so you can grow into your new role. When it comes to personal growth, you are always a student in the role of your life.

Make a list of the skills, or areas in your life that, if you made 10% improvement, would influence a positive impact in everything you do. Personal Growth is a commitment to what Tony Robbins calls CANI—a commitment to Constant and Never-Ending Improvement—that becomes the learning principle for your life. When you commit to a level of constant growth, it exponentially puts you ahead of the game.

When most people are "winding down" or settling into a comfort zone of lethargy (because that is what a comfort zone is) you are preparing yourself for the next challenge, the new learning curve coming up, and in this case, building a new set of experience into your life.

Your absolute commitment is the key. You refuse to give up or settle. You know the key is attitude, and every day can be put on reset. You don't get pulled into the past or held back by old systems and ways of thinking outdated decades past.

But many do, and it costs them. When you stop investing in your life at any age or level, the only option is to stay where you are as long as you can maintain this momentum or slide back. If you settle for where you are and what you have and are content with how far you have come, you will never know where you can go or who you can become. No limits. This is the mantra for personal growth.

"Whenever you see a successful person, you only see the public glories, never the private sacrifices to reach them."

– Vaibhav Shah

The most important person you can invest in is yourself. In fact, it's recommended by many personal development coaches to spend one hour a day on mindset training. This includes reading, meditating, or one hour of focused thinking such as visualization practice.

Invest the time in getting to know yourself. The investment you put into you should be a top priority. Why? You have to take care of yourself so you can be of service and benefit to others.

People who do regular maintenance on themselves are much happier and in a better position to invest more strongly in the world around them. When you're happy and have taken care of your basic needs, it fuels your motivation to invest in all other valuable relationships.

How much quality time do you spend on personal development? What is the one thing you have always wanted to do but haven't gotten around to? How would it make you feel if you could do it? What positive impact would it have on your other relationships?

We have unlimited resources today that you can tap into for personal growth. You don't even have to leave your home to learn a new skill or expand your knowledge. With the power of Internet and resources available in your own pocket, you are instantly connected to thousands of online courses, books, interviews, and media that has more than you need.

But it's important you apply what you focus on. Learning is the first stage of personal growth. Next is purpose of implementation. Is this knowledge or skill improving your life?

For example, you want to develop greater inner peace and connect at a deeper level with the universe. You learn to meditate and commit to 30 minutes a day for this practice. Or, you want to try a new job in a different industry, so you begin learning the various skills needed. Then you get a job in that industry and within several years have created a new skill and a new source of income.

But the best thing of all, and is the only level to measure your growth, is who you become through your commitment. You can literally transform your life within a few month or years by making your commitment to living the best life you can.

Whatever your goal is, decide what you want to become great at, and then the steps needed to get there. Commit to learning one new skill. People grow in different ways. Your meaning of personal growth is different from your friends or family. A mother wants to grow as a better parent, an employee wants to level up their skill to become better at work, and this has an influence on the amount of income they can grow into.

Decide the area you want to improve in and carve out that slice of time so you are putting in the time and effort. Growth can happen quickly or slowly, but if it's happening, that is what matters. The only way success can take hold is by asking yourself "How can I improve today by just 1%? What can I do differently now that I've never tried before?"

Challenge the obstacles that scare you. Do what is uncomfortable, and when you feel comfortable, do it again. This is how you expand your mind and your fear zone. You improve continuously by expanding your boundaries.

Incremental changes take time, but like the small steps to anything, are building blocks to growth. By committing to a 1% improvement plan, you can make consistent and gradual changes daily. If you continue to make daily increases in your performance, you will show significant gains in your skill set.

Too often, we focus on the big outcome—save $10,000 in one year, lose 20 pounds this month, or build a business in the next 30 days. But these goals result from small habits put into action each day.

"You will never change your life until you change something you do daily. The secret of your success is found in your daily routine."

— John Maxwell

Perform small habits consistently and you will grow in many areas of your life. Identify one area in your life you want to improve, and the daily habit required to achieve this goal. Make this a habit at the same time every day to study, grow and learn. Taking consistent action is the key.

We often miss these smaller improvements that make a difference. But the performance increase after months of refining and improving your system eventually leads to a rapid increase in quality and performance. A long-term focus on consistent action to get positive results leads to a successful outcome through ongoing diligence and commitment.

For instance, you can read for 30 minutes a day instead of watching television. You can work out, stretch or meditate instead of surfing the net or using your phone as you scroll endlessly looking for a mental fix. You can write 500 words in your journal instead of texting on social media. The reason most people don't make progress is lack of focus, clarity and consistently doing the habits that fail them.

Growth takes time and patience, but it's knowing what you should stop doing...and start doing. One habit I decreased by 90% was watching TV. Like many people, I'd turn on TV at night and put in 2-4 hours watching films or TV shows. It was out of habit and boredom. But I knew that to change, I'd have to either quit this or reduce the time spent.

I also played a lot of video games. By quitting games and saving TV for the weekends, I had a book written in one year. This became my launch pad for growth because it opened up other doors that would have otherwise been closed.

You can replace "write a book" with your #1 goal, or point of growth. You want to reach a deeper level of awareness through meditation? Make the time. You want to spend more time talking with your family and solving family issues? Make the time. You want to earn more money through setting up an online company? Learn and make the time.

There is no other way. Successful people who are committed to this path of constant learning and personal growth determined what they had to do to get there. They figured out the price to pay, and they paid it.

Shortcuts rarely work. You can travel the same path from A to Z as everyone else, and yet, you'll arrive at the destination before anyone else because they are working with a broken navigation system. How you get there depends on your level of commitment, and when you get there is determined by the amount of time you are willing to put into it.

What is the #1 area of your life that you've always wanted to become exceptional at? Decide. Commit to doing whatever it takes. Enjoy the process as you grow into your journey.

Here are 5 ways to invest in your personal growth:

1. **Hire a coach or mentor.** This can be a coach for your personal life or a business coach…or both! Working together with a coach can be the difference between success or failure.

   A great coach can help you work through difficult obstacles that you are blind to. Hire a coach and watch your life and business scale up.

2. **Scale up your skill.** Today, you have limitless resources at your fingertips to learn anything you need to do everything you want. You can enroll in online training courses that are in alignment with your goals. You can get courses, books and coaching on just about anything: Confidence building, email marketing, or learning SEO. Ongoing learning creates new opportunity!

   The only questions you have to ask are, "What is my goal, and what do I have to learn to achieve it?"

   Skill set is at the heart of success in everything. It trumps intelligence and pushes you into a growth mindset mentality.

3. **Read for one hour a day.** There are tons of books these days to help with your personal growth. The type of book you read depends on your goal. If you want to become better at personal productivity, I would recommend The One Thing.

If you are looking for a system to create a system of better habits, you can read *The Power of Habit* by Charles Duhigg. Books are the #1 resource for learning, but there are also courses, online Mastermind communities, and self-learning course platforms. The level of self-growth you can achieve is limitless!

4. **Invest in your health.** Set up a workout routine. You can run, lift weights, do yoga, or cross-fit. To maintain your health now means you could live a quality lifestyle well into retirement years.

I talk a lot about mindset in this book, but your body and health is critical. You need a healthy heart, organs, and functioning immune system to take full advantage of everything life has to offer. The body needs the mind, and your mind needs your body.

Get started with an exercise routine and do it first thing in the morning. If that isn't possible, get it done as soon as you can. Block in 30 minutes for your exercise routine, and make it a priority for the day.

5. **Create a life plan.** This is what your coach can help you with. You need a system of goals to direct you

towards your destination. Growth begins with having a goal. You can reflect on your goals in chapter XX on setting up Big Goals.

What should you invest in? This depends on your personal goals. You can focus on spiritual growth, financial investing, developing better job skills, or getting clear on your life's purpose.

- Personal growth is an ongoing investment. For every hour you spend on improving your lifestyle, the return on this investment is 10x. Or 100x.

- You can make exponential growth in your life and the lives of everyone you are in contact with by making personal growth a #1 priority.

- Build small habits into your daily routine. Make these habits consistent with your aim. If you skip a day, be sure to pick it up the next day.

Supercharge Your
Body

"The way you think, the way you behave, the way you eat, can influence your life by 30 to 50 years."

— *Deepak Chopra*

When it comes to physical exercise, this could easily be a series of books in and of itself. But this conversation is outside the scope of what this **Supercharge Your Best Life** covers, so I will keep it brief but pack this with enough information for you to get busy right now. I'll share with you my routine for working out and eating habits for the day.

You can follow all the great plans and do everything right, but if you fail to take care of your health, you won't be around to see the results of your planning.

As a disclaimer (you know this has to be said) always consult your doctor or physician before starting anything. If you need to lose weight, improve your cardio, or recover from an illness, there are other books and courses you can utilize. Visit your local physician for advice, or speak to a health and fitness expert before trying a new exercise or diet regimen.

With that being said, let's dive in.

Note: Portions of this material has been sourced from my book **Drive Your Destiny**. I have added exercises and relevant information so that you are learning what works and how best to apply.

Eating Well

Exercising on a regular basis is a great way to keep the weight off while boosting self-confidence. After a good workout, you'll feel great. To take it a step further, exercise in combination with a healthy diet not only boosts the quality of your life but also reduces the risk of disease. People who focus on their physical activity and back it up by eating the right foods can outperform anyone regardless of age and function at their best performance levels every day.

Just as the mind and spirit require mental nourishment to operate at peak effectiveness, the body requires a source of energy to function at its fullest capacity. Your mind requires positive thinking to stay healthy. When your body and mind are well-nourished, this contributes to the overall value and happiness found in each day.

Fueling Your System

A body that is nourished with the right foods will function longer, with increased mileage and little maintenance. If you load your system up with junk, you'll have less energy. To construct a sound body with mental and physical health, you need to focus on the quality of foods you take in as well as the size of the portions.

122 · SCOTT ALLAN

Knowing what to eat isn't sufficient enough; it is of vital importance to know *how much* to eat, and how to understand when your body has had enough. When we eat large quantities of foods from various food groups, the body breaks everything down and sorts it out. Some foods, such as fruits and vegetables, are digested and absorbed by the stomach quickly and efficiently.

Other foods take longer to break down and depending on how much you have eaten and in what combinations, the process requires considerable energy and time to digest everything.

Eating the foods we want, and in large quantities, feels enjoyable. However, after repeating this pattern for years and without giving any thought to the quality or quantity of the diet—not to mention the strange hours of the day that some people eat—our pleasure eventually turns to pain. This can result in stomach indigestion, heart disease, and obesity.

It is hard to believe that if we're not responsible, the food we eat can kill us someday. Remember the foods you consume can either improve the quality of your life, or completely ruin it. Whatever you eat, and how much, will impact how you feel.

If you're in the habit of eating loads of junk, you will feel sluggish. If you eat nutritious greens with the right amount of carbohydrates and proteins, you will feel ready to do anything. One style of eating gives you vital energy; the other approach kills this energy.

The key is to create healthy eating habits that support the lifestyle you desire. If you build these habits today, you will not only extend your life but, you will improve the quality of your life.

Eating well is a habit. However, before it can become a habit, you have to know what and how much to eat.

Reduce Your Intake

You do not have to eat large quantities out of habit or force; in fact, most people can get by on eating only sixty percent of what they normally consume. There's nothing to gain by eating a large meal at eight p.m. and then sitting down to watch TV for two hours. If you have ever done this—and I have—you might have awoken the next morning with that same food still in your stomach, barely feeling hungry.

Your body and your stomach has been asleep, so it hasn't had a chance to digest anything. Moreover, if you ate a heavy dinner, such as rice or meat and potatoes, it probably won't be fully digested until the next morning.

There's nothing wrong with eating below your hunger level. We eat when we're hungry or when it's time for dinner, and we usually eat until we've stuffed ourselves. You could actually eat only sixty percent of what you normally do and you would feel better and be just as active. More food is not always good. Massive food consumption causes the death of thousands of people every year.

The key is to listen to your body and not your mind. What is it telling you? What do you think it's craving? The mind is deceiving; its cravings are only based on the desire to consume. Have you ever found yourself eating even after your stomach was full? Your body didn't need the extra food, but the mind convinced you to eat. When you reach for a piece of cake or chocolate instead of fruit, is it your body that wants it, or is it the mind? Compulsive eating habits can create as much mayhem as any other habit.

Recommended healthy food intake includes fresh fruit and vegetables, meat, and dairy products. If you're a vegetarian, ensure you get enough protein through other means, such as beans and eggs. Avoid large quantities of junk.

Ten Power Tips for Healthy Eating

Power Tip #1: Eat plenty of vegetables and fruits every day. Include a dark green vegetable, such as broccoli, asparagus, or romaine lettuce, and an orange vegetable, such as carrots or sweet potatoes.

Power Tip #2: Every day, half of your consumption of grain products should be whole grain, such as brown and wild rice, bulgur, quinoa, or oatmeal.

Power Tip #3: Fish is high in protein and has little fat and few calories. Eat fish twice a week and you will keep your system clean while adding protein to your diet.

Power Tip #4: Include beans, lentils, and tofu (meat alternatives) more often in your diet. These are easily digested and are a terrific source of energy and vitality.

Power Tip #5: Drink lower fat milk and milk alternatives, such as fortified soy beverages. Be aware that other fortified drinks such as orange juice, and foodstuff such as rice, almonds, and potatoes, do not contain the same level of protein found in milk or soy.

Power Tip #6: Use unsaturated oils, such as canola, olive, and soybean as well as non-hydrogenated margarines. Include a small amount in your diet each day: 30 to 45 ml/2 to 3 tbsp.

Power Tip #7: Take a vitamin D supplement if you are over the age of fifty. Vitamin D, also known as the sunshine vitamin, is synthesized when sunlight hits the body. Vitamin D improves bone mineral density and builds stronger bones. A healthy intake of vitamin D lowers the risk of some cancers, multiple sclerosis, and reduces the risk of injury from falls or accidents.

Power Tip #8: Eat slowly. Take your time when eating. This helps with digestion and you'll enjoy your food more. People who eat too fast usually end up with indigestion and a stomachache.

Power Tip #9: Drink enough water. It's one of the best habits for cleaning out your system and keeping it operating at maximum performance. You don't have to drown yourself by drinking too much water, but remember to drink water when you're thirsty as opposed to bottled juice or a soft drink.

Power Tip #10: Eat breakfast every day! I believe breakfast is, as they say, the most important meal of the day. Also, the quality of the foods you eat in the morning sets the pace for the rest of the day.

If you eat a healthy mixture of fruits, your body will digest it easily and provide the greatest return in energy as water-based food. Fruits should be eaten on an empty stomach, as they are digested best this way. Fruit should never be eaten when you are completely full.

Building Health and Maximizing Energy

Besides eating well and breathing effectively, the third focal point is exercise. When you nourish the body by consuming healthy food, you build up a storehouse of energy that is released as soon as physical activity is applied.

Years ago, I discovered the benefits of lifelong dedication to physically training my body. There are almost too many benefits of a regular workout routine to list here. Regular exercise will not only enable you to keep the weight off, but you will also look good and feel great while building a storehouse of physical energy so that you can function at peak levels for maximum performance and efficiency.

There are many different forms of physical training. Some people prefer playing sports, whereas others enjoy yoga. There's bodybuilding or aerobics, swimming, running, or speed walking. Regardless of what you prefer, engaging in some form of activity at least twice a weak considerably boosts your energy levels.

A consistent exercise routine also builds confidence and contributes to the overall quality of your life. A balance of aerobic activity, light muscle training, and regular stretching with focused breathing techniques is all you need to build a solid physical foundation.

Aerobic Activity

Any exercise that concentrates on expanding the cardiovascular system is known as aerobic training, which includes swimming and running.

Whenever you perform an activity that creates the need for oxygen, it can be classified as an aerobic activity. Depending on the intensity of the exercise, it is categorized as moderate intensity or vigorous intensity aerobic exercise.

Aerobic Exercise in Moderation

Aerobic activity, when performed in moderation over a period of time, has the following benefits:

- Burns fat
- Increases the level of oxygen intake
- Increases the metabolic rate
- Creates a stronger and more efficient immune system
- Generates more energy
- Reduces the risk of heart disease by preventing the clogging of arteries

- Enhances performance in all areas of life
- Creates a foundation of learned discipline as the body is conditioned to stay in shape
- Enhances the body's ability to distribute oxygen to all vital organs

It takes approximately four to six months of consistent aerobic activity to build a strong, healthy foundation. If your exercise routine is irregular, you will fail to gain the real benefits of aerobic activities. For example, the benefit you'll get from running or swimming occasionally will be much less than what you can achieve by performing the same exercise consistently twice a week for six months. To make improvements, a regular routine is essential. It takes months of moderate exercise to develop a strong aerobic state.

If you were training for a triathlon, you wouldn't start running, swimming, and biking all in the same week. Doing so would only result in muscle injury and cause more harm than good. The key is in moderation over a sustained period.

Exercise is no different than practicing the piano; if you want to become a good pianist, you have to have a regular routine of practice. Over time, you'll develop the skills for the long term. Therefore, the key to staying healthy is to make exercise a part of your life. Make exercising regularly a priority for the long-term.

Consistent practice and making moderate adjustments to your exercise routine as you become stronger and more capable of handling a heavier physical workout is the key to success. Make your workouts a regular habit and keep altering your routine so that you don't become bored or stagnant.

Low-Intensity Exercise

This form of physical activity accelerates the heart rate and makes you breathe harder. It includes riding a bicycle, speed walking, or playing light sports that don't involve rigorous movements or extended running.

This type of exercise is fun and can be performed for an extended period over several hours with a lower heart rate. Although your breathing is hard, you can talk. In this state, you are burning oxygen, which creates a good aerobic condition. You will be able to burn fat more easily and generate a high level of sustained energy.

High-Intensity Exercise

This includes any sport or exercise that makes the heart race faster. By playing football, soccer, or basketball and being in constant motion, you burn sugar and stored fat.

It is recommended that you do not start training by throwing yourself into vigorous exercise. Your body needs to be conditioned to build up to a vigorous activity level. The intensity of this type of exercise needs to be altered according to age, as well. Now, here is the exercise routine I personally use to increase metabolism and stay lean and mean. But regardless what your goals are, you need to move. Movement is key to feeding your body and triggering neurochemicals such as dopamine and XXX

To learn more about exercise and the relationship to dopamine, check out this content created by Andrew Huberman at Huberman Labs.com.

Your Workout Program

You can workout and do all your training from home in 30 minutes a day or less without buying expensive gym memberships. I think going to the gym is great, because you are in the environment for training your body. But you can create this similar environment at home.

I promote working out at home IF you have the environment for it. You don't need much space and can make it work with just 7 feet of floor space

There are three items I use for this, and depending on your level of intensity, you can customize your training routine.

The only equipment you might want are:

- A heavy ball/medicine ball

- Dumbbell/weight set

- Pushup bars

Ideally, your body weight is enough for a full workout with a few weights to strap on if needed.

Here is what I do to get ready for working out.

Prep before sleep. Put out workout gear next to your bed the night before. Wake up and you're ready to go.

This includes a bottle of water. I know some people who actually go to bed IN their gym gear, so when they get up, it's GO time.

Decide your workout routine. What kind of routine or exercises? How many sets and reps? Set your exercise routine for 30 minutes.

Choose your space. The environment influences. The quality of your workout and concentration level

Preset your music playlist. Yes, you undoubtedly have your best tracks that you move quickly to. Preset everything and prepare your Air pods/Wireless headphones for jumping into training mode as soon as you wake up.

Set your alarm (the earlier the better). Wake up at a time that works best with your sleep cycle. I think it's best to not have the phone in the room when you're sleeping. You can use Alexa or Google Assistant to wake you up.

Do NOT Check email when you get up.

You want to minimize distractions from the moment you awaken. This is critical for focus, but impossible if you start the morning with jumping on social media or checking email. WE never just "check" to see what's going on, but from the moment you start clicking and swiping, all is lost.

Exercise Routine Example

- Warm up by taking a walk outside, walking up and down the stairs for five minutes, and follow up with stretching.

- Hold a plank position for 20-60 seconds. Increase the amount of time based on frequency of the exercise. The longer you continue to do this, the longer you can increase the time to do it.

- Push-ups: 10-15 repetitions. Try this with push up handles or flat palms.

- Squats: 10-15 repetitions (with dumbbell weights)

Rest for 30-40 seconds between sets and repeat. The number of sets you do will depend on your current fitness level. Last, cool down by walking on the spot and slowly stretch out your muscles.

Power Tips for Better Exercise

Warming up

The most common injury in sports is caused by a lack of stretching beforehand. A pulled muscle is often a result. One of the best ways to warm up before any exercise is to spend ten to fifteen minutes stretching. These are generally low-impact exercises to prepare the body for physical activity.

When you do this, focus on your breathing. Draw in deep breaths for a three-second count and exhale for four seconds. This expands your lungs and enhances your workout by improving the body's endurance ratio.

Cooling down

Cooling down after exercise is just as important as warming up, and it is a vital part of concluding a workout. This gives the body time to make the transition from a state of rapid exertion to a state of relaxation. The process of cooling down allows the body to normalize the breathing and heart rate.

During this phase, focus on light movements, such as stretching or walking. As we discussed earlier, this is a good time for breathing exercises, too. Finally, drink a glass of water to rehydrate.

Staying hydrated

Water replenishes your body with essential minerals that allow it to run properly, which will increase your chances of achieving your exercise goals. Make sure you always have a bottle of water at a workout.

Focus on eating complex carbohydrates before a workout.

Glucose is your body's most essential source of fuel. Your pre-workout meal should be comprised of complex carbohydrates. Ensure this is a small meal, and wait at least one hour for the food to be converted into energy to be used while training.

If you are doing moderate aerobics, just a light snack with a short waiting time before exercise is sufficient. For complex workouts, eat carbohydrates with a light protein combo, and lengthen your waiting period. Bread, vegetables, or pasta are recommended food items for a pre-workout meal.

Post-workout meal

The meal consumed after exercise is as important as the meal consumed before the workout. First, you should typically try to eat within an hour after your training, and make it proteins and carbohydrates. Avoid fats of any kind. Eating fats in this phase slows the digestion process of the carbs and proteins.

The size of this meal depends on your body weight. For more information, visit Canada's Food Guide. It will provide you with a more detailed approach, complete with tables and a personal tracking system for recording everything you consume.

Planning Your Workout

During the next week, you are going to record the food you eat. Note how you feel after the food you consume. Are you full of energy or do you feel sluggish? Did you have a balance of vegetables today? What time did you eat dinner, and what did you eat?

By listening to your body and your stomach, you can gauge how certain foods affect you. You can keep track of what and how much you eat by using "My Food Guide Servings Tracker" in the Canadian Food Guide.

Workout Plan and Training – If you check the Internet or your local bookstore, you will find a wide resource of workout routines and schedules for just about anything you're interested in. It really depends on how you want to exercise and what you want to do.

Another alternative is to visit your local gym and see what they have to offer. Although you can generally train for free at home without spending money, many people like the motivational atmosphere of going to a gym. You can also get a free consultation on training and dieting. Set up a workout routine that coincides with your health and fitness goals.

Supercharge Your
Goals

"By recording your dreams and goals on paper, you set in motion the process of becoming the person you most want to be. Put your future in good hands—your own."

— Mark Victor Hansen

As Lewis Carroll stated, *"If you don't know where you're going, you'll probably end up somewhere else."*

Your goals provide you with a sense of direction and are the blueprints to construct the reality of your dreams. Goals provide clarity. Without a concise plan, we shift from one idea to the next. Our dreams become lofty prospects that never materialize into anything concrete. Once you know where you are going, it is much easier to reach your destination when you have a clear line of sight ahead, driven by a system of progressive steps to get you there.

A master goal constructs the building blocks for a prosperous future. By creating a system of goals that inspire and motivate you to engage in positive action, you plant the roots of success and design a system for success that brings every opportunity imaginable.

By setting up a life goal (master goal), you take the guesswork out of "where's my life going?" Not only that, but you reduce your chances of failing later in life, and exponentially increase your SUCCESS factor!

The Rise of Big Goals

The key to creating a master goal is to set a goal so extraordinary that it challenges all of your limited beliefs and thoughts. These goals are so big, they make you have serious doubts about achieving them. Your first reaction is to disbelieve YOU could ever accomplish this master goal. You are asking yourself, "How can I achieve this goal in this lifetime?"

These goals are also known as BHAG (Big Hairy Audacious Goals) as coined by business author Jim Collins in his groundbreaking book, "Built to Last."

Jim Collins needed to create a phrase that scared the pants off of business leaders. It had to be exciting, challenging, and portray a system of goals too big to be achievable. The risk of failure would be high.

Here is an example. Two people set financial goals to earn a certain amount of money in the next year. One person sets the goal to double their income in the next two years from $60,000 to $120,000. It is a tough goal. Not impossible, but difficult. Someone else decides to take their monthly income from 60k a year to one million a year, but this goal is set for ten years.

Now, if you look at these 2 goals, the BHAG is, of course, to reach one million a year. One goal is tough to make happen but doable. The other appears impossible to make it real and is planned out over the long-term. Your Master Goal is your pillar objective that takes 5-10 years at least to get results.

The goal has to be so big that you ask yourself:

· "Is this possible?"

· "Am I aiming for too much?"

· "If I don't make this, what does it mean?"

· "Is anyone else doing this? Should I scale this down?"

Most people hesitate to set Big Goals. They are uncomfortable. We are educated to think logically, inside the box, and to go for the low-hanging fruit. Why take a risk for the treasure at the top of the mountain, when you can gather up all the easy nuggets below without making the climb?

All great accomplishments were driven by scary goals (also known as Big hairy Audacious Goals, as described by Jim Collins/author of Good to Great).

NASA put humans on the moon. Nike launched a global corporation that beat Adidas. Microsoft put computers on every desk and in every home. Every achievement that seemed impossible became possible by hard work, organization, setting micro-tasks, and a target-oriented quantitative or qualitative goal.

If you are willing to Fail Big, you are ready to take your dreams to the stars...and beyond.

But let me ask you this...what goal can you think of right now that excites you? You are so charged up that you can't sleep, in part from fear, but also knowing you're taking a path that shocks most people. When you talk about it, your friends just say, "Good luck with that." In other words, "That can't possibly happen, but I'll play along."

Your Master Goal—Big Hairy Audacious Goal—is more than just your average run-of-the-mill objective you accomplish with a few months of hard work. It is a goal so big and scary that the possibility of making it real challenges all of your limiting beliefs.

The Master Goal breaks small thinking around all your beliefs. It challenges your mind to push out of the box of limitations and form new beliefs targeted to achieve what most people would label "impossible".

Your master goal is the blueprint for your life. It is not just a one-time moment of achievement. After your moment on stage is over, you can continue on to the next goal. And the next one. Your life will become a roadmap for others to aspire to.

Here is a 12-point checklist for setting up your master goals I alternatively will use the term Big Goals). Every super achiever—from sports heroes to musicians and writers and actors and business entrepreneurs— started with a master goal. Committed to paper, the goal becomes real.

You don't have to be a super-achiever to achieve your dreams. You just have to have a plan, work at it, and wake up each day thrilled knowing you are moving your dreams forward and building your best life.

The 12-Point Goal System for Building a Master Goal

(1). Create Your Dream List. For the next thirty minutes, write down everything you've always wanted to have, do, be, and experience in your lifetime. Don't worry about how crazy it sounds. If it scares you, that's even better. Don't think too hard about how you'll accomplish these things. You can do this in a linear note taking style with bullet points, or, use the mind map approach.

(2) Identify Your Master Goal.

Your big goal (Master Goal for Life) must have a transformational impact on your journey. Knowing with specific intent what you really want and must have is the first concrete step to making it happen. Once you set your sights on a target, you commit your goal to paper by writing it down and making it real. Then, you will design a step-by-step plan for success to take you through to achieving your master goal.

Your #1 Master Goal has to be the one thing in life you have always desired the most. It is your grandest adventure, a seemingly insurmountable obstacle that scares you as much as it excites you. It brings everything in your life into direct alignment with the great purpose that governs all things.

Right now, take a few minutes to visualize your master goal. If you know what it is, write it down on paper. Continue to write it down as many times as you want to. Don't worry about the details of your master goal, or how you are going to achieve this.

Remember, this is the BHAG that scares you. Is your goal to earn an extra $10,000 next year, or an extra $1,000,000? Do you want to take a trip to Alaska for two weeks, or travel the world for 6 months? Is your goal to change your job to a better one that pays an extra $5,000 a year, or start your own company and bring in $5 million per year consistently over the next ten years?

You have to create goals that are worthy of your failure. It is the Mount Everest of your life, and your mission—everything you strive to do from this day forward—is targeted towards making it happen. You will either reach the peak of your dreams, or fail trying.

When it comes to a master goal, your first thought should be "How can I achieve this? It seems so radical. Nobody would attempt this." Yes, it should be. That's why they are big and scary. Anyone can knock off a goal that is attainable, but it's the BHAG that makes you shake and cause others to look at you in disbelief (and doubt) when you tell them your plans.

(3). Attach a Timeframe to Your Master Goal.

A deadline reminds you that something requires your immediate attention. Without a deadline, you are leaving the door open for procrastination—and believe me, it will come in and take over your life if you let it. Once you affix a timeframe to your goal, it becomes more real than you could possibly imagine.

No matter how far into the future your dream is, always attach a timeframe. A workable timeframe is the anchor that holds the goal in place. Without it, your dreams and enthusiasm will drift away. You can set this goal for anywhere from 5 years to 20 years. Most BHAG have a minimum of ten years before they are completed. You might be thinking "but that's such a long time." Yes, it is, but anything worthwhile requires a lifetime of commitment.

With a big goal, your master dream for life, it could take you 5-20 years to reach this. Even then, there will be another plateau to leap for. There will be many. But we are not concerned with plateau #2 until we hit the first one. You have to conquer your "Everest" first, and then you can turn your attention towards landing on the moon.

Action task:

Attach a completion date to your master goal. Will it take you 5 years? 10 years? 20 years?

(4). Create a "First-Year" Set of Goals for Your Master Goal

A master goal without planned intentional action becomes a dream or a wish. We need massive action to move our goal forward and start building momentum. To be living your dream in a decade, you have to start now. You have to create a set of smaller goals for the year, the quarter, and eventually, break it down to smaller weekly tasks.

For your master goal, make a list of "first-year" goals you will work towards. Let's take an example. We will use someone called Harry who has a master goal to build a fifty-million-dollar real estate business focused on selling high-end homes valued over $5 million.

Harry's first-year goals are:

1. Hire three top-level agents

2. Open two branches in three states

3. Build out profit for the first year to $5 million.

You can create as many first-year goals as you want to, but keep in mind, they must be attainable and achievable. I keep my yearly goals to three big goals, but each goal is broken down into monthly and weekly tasks, too.

Then, for every year you are working on your business, you create a list of goals and break each down into sub goals.

(5). Build Out Master Goal "Sub-Goals"

Sub goals contribute to the overall completion of a larger goal. Your plan of action will involve many steps that lead to the success of each goal. These steps for success may include research, making phone calls, or sending out applications.

In basic terms, your plan is like a to-do list. It is a list of step-by-step tasks to achieve your goal. By breaking down the steps for each goal, you can manage the time allocated to making progress towards each one.

Action Task:

Write down a set of action steps for each goal. Post these action steps in a visible place.

(6). Visualize the Success of Your Goals.

If you are to create the life and results you desire, develop a practice of imagining and visualizing yourself as already being a success. How do you feel? What has changed in your life? How different do you feel as a person? How did you grow and change by achieving your goals?

From professional sports to the executive boardroom, every successful achievement is made possible if there is a vision to build it.

Think of your success as having already happened, and your subconscious mind will bridge the gap between the two worlds of the present and what is yet to come.

Action Task: Block in twenty minutes in the morning and perform a "visual clarity" exercise. You must get clear on the vision you have for your life. This can be a vision for the next year or five years. But begin by building it in your mind. What your mind can imagine, your actions will create in the real world.

(7). Join a Mastermind Community

This could be a group of accountability partners or people who can support you on your journey. Mastermind groups are critical to staying connected, inspired and, when you need it, to provide feedback on your strategic planning.

For years, I struggled to hit my goals. I failed at deadlines most of the time and didn't enjoy the process of goal-setting but finding a mastermind group changed all that. Your accountability partner or mastermind group can:

· Check in on your progress each week

· Send daily reminders of the master tasks you are working on for the day, week and year

· Help you celebrate when you reach the goal that has taken you weeks, months, or years to achieve

· Provide solutions to help you break through tough obstacles.

Accountability is a great way to stay on track and motivated when you are stuck in procrastination mode, and it gives you the opportunity to talk to someone about your objectives. Find an accountability partner/mastermind group to work with, and you will not only hit your most important goals, but you'll enjoy the process.

Successful people who remain undefeated are those who can network and create successful teams of people who are willing to support each other.

Action task:

Identify the people who can help you with your goals. Then, ask yourself, "How can we help each other succeed?" Look for these people, and when you find them, build your mastermind team of influencers.

(8). Expand on Action Tasks for Your Master Goal

In this step, you will break each action task into smaller steps so they are easier to tackle. By breaking them down, you are giving yourself manageable chunks to work with, while reducing stress.

By breaking down the goal into sizeable chunks, it will be easier to track your success. These smaller steps could include making phone calls, arranging a meeting, or doing research on a subject.

Expand on the action tasks for your #1 goal. Go back to the mind-mapping strategy and write down as many tasks as you can think of—even if they are months away.

Action task:

Make a list of action tasks for your #1 Master Goal.

(9). Prioritize Action Steps (and do one thing only.)

Now that you have your list of action tasks, put these in order of importance. What needs to be done today? This week? Within the next three months?

Take five minutes every night before bedtime to write down the one task you will complete the following day. This is a powerful habit. By doing one thing every day, it pushes your goal closer to the finish line.

Taking massive action really means acting consistently. So, every day, you must do something that moves the needle.

At the start of every day, write down the ONE action task that will move you closer towards your goal. This isn't a to-do-list. It is one thing only you must work on until finished.

Action task:

Prioritize your action steps.

(10). Identify the Obstacles Blocking Your Progress

As with anything, there will be challenges and obstacles to work through. Identify three immediate challenges you will encounter while working towards your goals. This usually comes down to one of three things—or, it could be all three:

1. You lack necessary information. Is there anything you need to know to move ahead? Do you need to take a course, do an interview, or call somebody?

2. A lack of resources. You might need something such as money to continue your goal, but remember, you are limited not by resources but by a lack of resourcefulness. This means you can find a way to make it work and get more money. Maybe you need to convince someone to help you, such as a mentor or coach.

3. Your values are confused. There are times when our values are not in alignment with the goals we are pursuing. This requires us to evaluate the values driving us.

Whatever barriers are in our way, there is a way to get through it. Work out the solutions and create an action plan to chip away at the weaknesses.

Action task:

Identify the barriers that could hold you back.

(11.) Identify the Knowledge and Skills needed to achieve your goal. You most likely will have to learn one or several key skills to succeed. Ask yourself, "What is the one skill I need to succeed in this area?" Now, there are probably several skills you need. So identify what you must know, and the skills you can hire other people for. Outsourcing and delegating is critical to prevent overwhelm and frustration for not making progress.

Action Task:

Write down this skill, and how much time you are willing to commit to mastering this. How long will it take you to learn this skill? Is this something you must do, or can you hire someone to perform this task?

(12). Review Your Progress (Weekly Planning Sessions)

This is probably the most vital step to effectively manage your goal portfolio. By reviewing your goals on a regular basis, you can easily recognize and monitor your progress. During the review process, you will:

· Identify pending obstacles blocking your path

· Review and update your action checklist of tasks required to achieve your goal(s)

· Assess your progress and consider whether your deadline is manageable

· Add any new thoughts or ideas to support your continued progress.

It is easy to get pulled away from the work you really want to do, but most of our distractions can be managed easily. The reason is most distractions are self-created. Of course, you will always have family situations come up, or a friend drop by who needs something. This is where blocking off time each day to get your work done and put time into your project is critical.

One major distraction many people have is negative or fragmented thinking. Our mind wants to do one thing, while our will wants to do another.

This is when concentration comes into play. When you concentrate on something, you make it your most important priority. You focus your energy on the task and then concentrate to make sure it is done correctly, and you are doing only those things required to move closer to your goals.

Action Task

Review the progress you are making once a week. Take note of the areas in which you are failing and try to tighten them up.

Are you striving to fulfill any life goals? Is there a dream you always wanted to work toward, but the fear of getting started is keeping you stuck? Do you have lofty goals that aren't going anywhere?

Confident people have challenging goals that inspire them to work hard and fulfill their lifelong dreams. They have a set direction and every action they take, every decision they make, and the level of fulfillment experienced is directly linked to the goals set for life. People with goals are more focused, highly motivated, and opportunistic.

Once you know where you are going, it is much easier to reach your destination when you have a clear line of sight ahead, driven by a system of progressive steps designed to get you there.

Here is a simple 9-point system to build your life-changing goals.

1. Write down your priority goal. This is your Master Goal. It is the one thing you must have more than anything.

2. Define your why. Why is this goal important? What would happen if you didn't achieve this goal? Write down your biggest reason WHY you must have this one thing.

3. Mind map the action steps needed to turn this goal into a tangible reality. You can use the free app SimpleMind Lite or the paid app Mindjet.

4. Put the action steps you are working on in order. What is the next step? You can use the Todoist app to track your progress and action steps.

5. Review your progress at the end of each week. What did you achieve? What area of the goal process is giving you resistance?

6. Visualize yourself as already succeeding. How do you feel? How will your life level up after achieving your goal?

7. Set a deadline for reaching your first milestone. You can set mini-milestones for each action item.

8. Establish your action plan for each week at the beginning of the week.

9. Find an accountability partner. Work with this person to help each other reach

   your goals.

Action Plan: Create Your Goal Portfolio Action Plan

Set aside thirty minutes each day to work on your action plan. By committing to a specific time block, you can make progress every day, even in small increments. The little steps add up over time. Reward yourself for the small steps you accomplish on the way to completing your goal. Once you have succeeded, decide the next master goal and continue to build toward your dream.

Now that you have a set of action steps for planning your goals, it's time to write about them.

Exercise in Goal Writing

For the next sixty minutes, write down everything that you have always wanted to be, do, have, and experience in your lifetime. Don't worry about how crazy it sounds. If it scares you, that's even better. Don't think too hard about how you are going to accomplish these things, no matter how ridiculous they may be.

Write down the places you want to go, the skills you want to master, what you want to learn, who you want to meet, and what you desire to build and create. Make a list of all the things you have dreamed of doing but never did because you couldn't find the time, energy, or motivation.

Once you are finished, hold on to this list. Tack it up on your wall. Make it visible. Review your goals at least once a day. Focus on one goal at a time and when you're finished, move on to the next one.

Supercharge Your
Emotions

"If your emotional abilities aren't in hand, if you don't have self-awareness, if you are not able to manage your distressing emotions, if you can't have empathy and have effective relationships, then no matter how smart you are, you are not going to get very far."

— Daniel Goleman

One of the most direct ways to master your emotions is to take control over your thoughts. Every emotion is accompanied by a thought at first. You must understand that, to control your emotions, you must think about the feelings you want to experience.

The one question you must ask yourself is: "What set of actions must you take to feel the way you want to feel?"

In the study of neuroscience, we now know that our brain connects physical patterns to the habits we engage in regularly. So, if your habit is to get angry or lose your temper suddenly, that behavior is recorded, and it gets more powerful the more you exercise it.

The concept of emotional mastery was first introduced in the 1960s with the Schachter-Singer experiment, where researchers gave participants a shot of a placebo "vitamin." Participants then observed colleagues complete a set of questionnaires. When the colleagues responded angrily to the questionnaires, the observing participants experienced anger in turn. But when the colleagues responded happily, the participants also experienced a happy feeling. The study's results implied a connection between peer influence and the felt experience of emotion.

Now, think about the thought patterns you have that are directly linked to your emotions. If you lock into the same emotional pattern every day, multiple times per day, you are creating a powerful bond that becomes unbreakable. This is true if you are experiencing thoughts of anger, sadness, depression, or fear.

What thoughts do you regularly have that create feelings of fear or anger? Are these thoughts repetitive? Write them down:

Your thoughts about a thing will create the emotions. How you respond to external stimuli is mirrored internally and you attach a belief to the experience. If this is a negative emotion you want to stop having, the only way to break it down is to break the pattern of thought and begin building a new neuro pathway.

Since emotions are a product of your experiences—and how we perceive those experiences—you can cultivate positive emotions by focusing in on them.

Here is an example. Think about a situation—or person—that makes you become angry. You feel like breaking something. Your jaw clenches and you ball your fists. Your head feels ready to explode.

At this moment, observe what you are thinking about. Is it a situation you don't like? A person that has wronged you or did something to make you angry?

By the way, nobody can make you angry. Your thoughts and sense of perception can only control this.

Now, shift your thoughts to this situation and put it in a different light. If it is a situation or institution causing you grief, imagine all the people who work there. See them going to work every day to earn money for their families. If it is a person you are angry against, think about that person's life and all the things he or she probably does for family and friends.

Now, how do you feel? Still angry? Make a note of the thoughts you had that made you experience this anger in the first place. AS you think differently about the situation, your emotions change with it. The situation hasn't changed, only your observation of the event. One pathway leads to suffering of the mind, and the other path frees it.

You are learning to control your thoughts. And in doing so, you control your emotions. This is why the search for happiness is futile. You already know how to be happy. You create the thoughts that create happiness.

You generate thoughts that bring sadness and anger. The question is, "How do you want to feel right now?"

"When our emotional health is in a bad state, so is our level of self-esteem. We have to slow down and deal with what is troubling us, so that we can enjoy the simple joy of being happy and at peace with ourselves."

— Jess C. Scott

Step One: Catch the Trigger Thought or Image

This step involves catching your thoughts when they latch onto a negative idea. Think of it this way: When you watch the same movie again and again, the movie itself never changes. It is the same film every time. Our thoughts can act like the scenes of a movie, replaying without change and reinforcing limited beliefs with each replay.

When your thoughts latch onto a negative idea or image, what is it? Is this the same thought you have every day? Is it around relationships, money, or the future?

Step Two: Cut the Limited Thought Pattern

Over the course of years, we buy into the limitations that define our emotions and actions. When you catch your thoughts that are playing the same movie reels over and over, then it's like taking a pair of scissors and cutting that film.

When you find yourself trapped in a negative thought loop, visualize taking a pair of scissors and cutting the film in two. You are ending the thought that is creating negative emotions.

Cut your visual image with your imaginary scissors. This puts a stop to the internal ranting. You are free to recreate the scene.

How do you feel after doing this?

Step Three: Repeat this Process

If something works, try it again. Continue to practice it until you can shift your emotions at will. Your emotions are powerful and make or break you.

By realizing how quickly you can change your own state, you add a new level of confidence to your personal mastery. You are no longer a victim to circumstances or other peoples' mood swings. You are not affected by another's bad day. Someone's anger doesn't become your anger.

Describe your feelings after you have "cut" your negative thoughts.

Emotional mastery does not mean shutting down or denying your feelings. Instead, learning how to master your emotions means appreciating them as a part of yourself. Your emotions are not "wrong" but, are simply a state of being.

To master your emotions, build confidence by rehearsing handling situations where this emotion might come up in the future. Visualize yourself handling the situation when it occurs. Imagine your emotions as you can guide your feelings to create the experience you want to have.

Now, think about something that makes you happy: working on a passion project, a childhood memory, or spending time with your friends, family, or children. You can feel your emotions shifting from rage to a happy, jovial feeling. Concentrate on these thoughts as long as you can, and you will permanently change your state.

What emotions are you experiencing?

The ability to change your state of mind is the most powerful strategy you can implement today. The one reason people are so unhappy is because they are stuck in a state of mind that is controlling their emotions. They latch onto an idea or a negative thought that is all-encompassing, and it consumes them.

This is how people become agitated, depressed, or even suicidal. They can't break out of their negative thought patterns. They feel hopeless. Helpless. They have nothing to live for. Life becomes an exhausting loop and we just want it to stop. In many cases, people need help, intervention, or just someone to talk to about how they are feeling.

Your emotional state is always in your control. We can't stop people from acting, saying, or being the way that they are. They are running their own show, and it usually has nothing to do with you. But when people—whether they be family members, co-workers, or strangers—do something that affects our emotional state, we take it personally.

If you want to master your emotional state, you will have to start with bringing your thoughts into the present moment. Calm down the screaming mind.

Describe the thoughts you will create when you catch yourself in a negative frame of mind?

Eliminating Resentment

> "Any person capable of angering you
> becomes your master."

— Epictetus

One of the greatest causes of misery is failing to resolve resentments linked to past events. Holding on to anger and bitter feelings of the past instigates a cycle of negative emotional trauma. Resentment is a form of negative energy that eats away at us over time, leading to depression, anxiety, and other negative emotions.

Taking on resentment is like swallowing a bitter pill. You are linking the pain and suffering of the past to the thoughts and emotions of the present. Bitter, deep-seated anger and resentment builds over the years. A resentment will erode away all chances of leading a happy, fulfilling life as your thoughts are consumed by focusing on the shortcomings of another. This could be a friend, family member or company co-worker that has wronged you.

Resentment robs you of the present by focusing on the past. You hold onto your pain by refusing to let it go, as if you have the right to be angry. The wounds never have a chance to heal. In fact, over time, this pain can cause severe mental trauma and illness.

If you're holding onto a resentment right now, ask yourself if it has made your life any better. Would you really feel better if you could exact some kind of justice, or get even?

To be emotionally free, you must target any resentments you have, and concentrate to heal your mind from any grudges you're holding onto.

By identifying your resentments, you free yourself from the emotional suffering they are causing.

Do you feel any resentment no towards a particular person? If yes, what is the reason?

Do yourself a favor and find a way to get over the pain caused by past events. I am not suggesting that you try to forget these painful events, but how you choose to deal with them is entirely up to you. The grief you're holding onto is your responsibility. It is time to let go, move on, and live your life.

Taking Inventory of Your Resentments

I created a "resentment inventory" and included the names of the people and events I resented as well as the reason behind my resentment. Here are six steps to help you prepare your resentment inventory.

Here are the steps for working through any resentment you are hanging on to:

(1). Create a resentment list. Make a list of all the people, places, events, and/or principles that you resent. Make your list here:

(2). List the causes. Now, go back to the top of the list and in another column or on a separate piece of paper, write down the cause of the resentment for each item. Why are you angry? What happened?

(3). Identify the negative impact. How has this resentment affected you? Next, write down how each event affected you. Did it impact your wealth, self-esteem, emotional state, or security?

(4). Identify the payoff of your resentment. What is the benefit of holding on? Most people feel they are gaining something by resenting the source of their pain. Write down what you are gaining from continuing to hold onto your resentment.

(5). Identify how you keep the resentment going. What is your role in this situation? As someone who has been wronged, you might think you are the victim and therefore take no responsibility. What thoughts are you harboring that feed into this? How do you continue to hand over your personal power to the source of your resentment?

(6). **How are you contributing to the situation?** The people or institutions that you dislike, regardless of the reasons, are not going to change. This leaves you with only one choice: you must change your perceptions and attitude. Let others change theirs. You have the personal power to evolve beyond your present condition.

(7) **Reverse your thoughts with forgiveness**. This is a difficult step. But it is the key to resentment recovery. When your resentment crops up, frame it in a new window. Give thanks to the person whom you are holding resentment towards for the lesson they have taught you. Send out a wish for this person's success and well-being.

(8) **Focus on people you love and appreciate.** The previous step is a challenge. If you find yourself stuck, always remember to think about the people in your life that mean the most to you: Good friends, family or people that serve your favorite coffee every morning. Work on step 8 and give it time.

Who are the people in your life that matter most?

(9). **Take inventory regularly.** Do an inventory of your resentments every 2—4 weeks. Check for new resentments that may have cropped up and use these steps for dealing with them.

Do you have any deep-seated resentment toward a person, place, or event that happened in your life? How can you release this resentment and anger? Does it make you feel good to harbor this resentment or do you feel a deep sense of suffering? Follow the steps mentioned in this chapter to conduct a regular inventory every few months.

Write about a major life event or relationship from the past. How did this change you?

How much time and energy do you spend thinking about past events, trauma, and relationships? Do these memories fill you with positive or negative energy? How do you feel about your life in general?

Are you deeply satisfied with where you are today? If the answer is no, what are you going to do about it?

If you were given the chance to alter any past event or deed, what would it be?

Why would you choose to change this event?

If this event hadn't occurred, would your life be different today?

If so, how would it be different? More importantly, how do you know your life would have turned out better?

Disengaging Your Negative Emotions

If you want to master your emotional state, begin with bringing your thoughts into the present moment. Calm down the screaming mind. Doesn't it feel like your mind is screaming at you sometimes?

In your efforts to shut it down, you turn on the TV or drown your thoughts in loud music. But that rarely helps. It just creates a distraction. As soon as the TV show is over, you are back to the root of your problem. The negative voices are back and stronger than ever.

"Too often we underestimate the power of a touch, a smile, a kind word, a listening ear, an honest compliment, or the smallest act of caring, all of which have the potential to turn a life around."

— Leo Buscaglia

What you need to do is to break the pattern. Engage your negative thinking and the screaming voices in your head. They are not running the show as you have been deceived into thinking. It is all you. It is your show, and you are the director of your own performance. The time is now to stand up and take charge.

You can change your emotions at any time. By creating a new system of thoughts when negative emotions come up, you can create the emotional state you really want by taking intentional action. This is the better alternative to just "letting emotions take over."

Negative thinking doesn't just happen without your permission. This is an important lesson to learn. You give yourself permission to think, feel, and react.

Negative thinking evolves from fear and discontent. Your thoughts are latching onto a negative experience you've had leading to resentment or regret. If it is the future, your negative emotions are caught in worry or fear of the unknown.

These emotions and thoughts are natural, and it isn't about ridding yourself of these emotions. That's an impossible task because they are a part of you. But managing your thinking so that you are the one creating a state of positive self-love.

Identify with what you're feeling. To take that step toward emotional mastery, ask yourself:

- *What am I really feeling right now?*

- *Am I really feeling...?*

- *Is it something else?*

Appreciate and acknowledge your emotions. The emotions you have are not good or bad. They are just happening. Acknowledge what you're feeling. This is how you communicate with yourself and you never what to make it "wrong."

Don't shut down your emotions. Seek to find the message they are conveying. Why are you experiencing this emotion? Ask yourself questions about the emotions:

What happened recently to trigger my emotions this way?

What am I going to do about this? Do I want to continue feeling this way?

Believe you have the power to change this. You are not at the mercy of your emotions. You are the master of emotions when you choose to be.

Your life is a reflection of your thoughts.

Think of a time when you felt this emotion in the past. What did you do about it at that time? Repeat the process you used before if it worked. You can work with affirmations, journaling or doing an activity that gets you moving. Change your state with action.

Believe you can handle this emotion when it comes up. Build emotional confidence by rehearsing handling situations where this emotion might come up in the future. visualize, hear and feel yourself handling the situation. Train your mind to feel less about the motion and take confident action.

Remember the negative consequences of feeing into this emotion. If you don't change it, you lose time when it's spent trapped living in your negative emotions. Observe the mental suffering you created in the past by allowing this emotion to rule you.

Build excitement and anticipation. Celebrate your ability to master your emotions by getting really excited about the process to change it. You have the personal power to make this emotional shift. Do it now!

Remove Negative Internal Language

How many negative phrases can you count in a day? I'll bet you have as many as I do, and I can catch myself on many of them. But what makes these negative connotations stick is that we justify being used or abused.

- "If only he/she would stop…."

- "I can't believe they did that. Now I'm screwed."

- "Nothing ever works out for me. I told you so."

- "He makes me so angry."

- "Everything would be so perfect if only…."

- "All I want is (fill in your desire here) and then I'll be happy."

- "See how much she has, and look at how little I have?"

- "Life just isn't fair."

- "Some people have all the luck."

By playing the victim, you place yourself in a position of power. You want to be right and they are wrong. You want to be understood while the misunderstanding lies with the other person. You want an apology for being wronged so you can justify how right you always are.

Here is what I do. Carry a small notebook with you. You can use a tablet, but I prefer actual paper because digital material gets lost easily.

Throughout the day, when you start to complain or use one of your negative phrases, write it down. Right there. This will make you aware of what you are thinking and saying that keeps your self-pity train moving.

Self-pity is another form of negative thought. It spins a web of lies that tell us, "If I am the victim, I don't have to do anything."

Use your notebook to identify the phrases you use. Then, add up the phrases you have most commonly used. Everybody has several that they love to use repeatedly.

Supercharge Your Emotions with Daily Journaling

To connect with your emotions, write about them. Journaling is a powerful habit to get you connected to your thoughts and emotions.

Journaling has become a way of practice that I would highly recommend you start doing.

Why journaling? First of all, it pulls your ideas and thoughts out of your head and gets them down on paper. It's impossible to see what is going through your mind until you lay everything down on paper.

Journaling is a healthy (and fun) way to keep track of your progress. It is a path detailing your journey from here to there. It's not how far you have to go that you should be focused on but rather, how far you have come on this path.

One small positive thought in the morning can change your whole day.

Journaling has been a best practice for many successful artists and business people to track their journey through the years of change.

In this journal, you can make it daily or weekly. I keep a daily journal that I write in twice a day, once at the beginning of the day in the morning and again in the evening. But in my journal, I do have a list of my best three goals. I would recommend that, no matter what you are using, your goals are listed first.

The other content for the journal is inspirational thoughts you had throughout the day or positivity quotes. I include sketches of mind maps or simple blueprints for my business. Your journal serves its purpose best by using it as a therapy guide.

Instead of Netflix before bed, make journaling in your freedom journal ten minutes before bed your #1 habit. It keeps you focused, generates new ideas, and moves you in the direction your purpose is intending.

You can break their journal writing up into various sections: goals, inspirational thoughts and quotes/affirmations, or morning pages written first thing in the morning as a way to wake up your mind.

You can include a gratitude section and list your daily gratitude for that day. How you structure it is up to you.

The journal is best used when your mind is at peace, either after meditation or at the end of a day when the work is finished and you've had time to wind down.

In my journal, I keep my primary goals at the front on the first page. But I write them down every morning on a desk pad. I start the day off by writing down my goals. It is a powerful habit that gets you focused, and streamlines all actions to steer towards that goal.

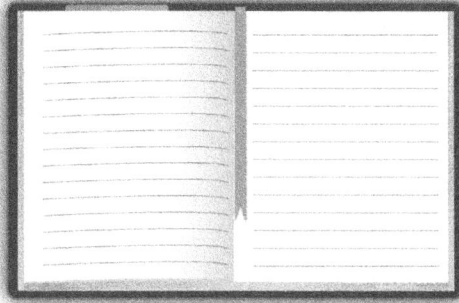

I love journaling and consider it to be an important part of my day. To have a great experience with your journaling journey, I have a few suggestions:

1. **Use a physical journal.** I know, we can journal on Word or Evernote, but, it's not the same as taking physical notes and being able to get creative. You don't get the same effect with notes on your phone because it lacks that feeling of "I created something!"

Digital material gets buried under all the other digital notes you're taking. But an actual journal you can keep on your desk and it's always there as a reminder.

2. **Use sticky Notes.** I love sticky notes, and they are great for making notes you really want to stand out in your journal. Use sticky notes for writing down important quotes, or your goals for that day, week or year.

3. Begin with your "Thoughts for the Day". I start my journal with a one page thought of the day. This could be from something I've read or ideas I had to achieve my critical goal. Make a short list of topics you can start writing about in your first journal session.

Here are ten prompts to get you started:

1. What would your ideal day look like?
2. What is one thing you've always wanted to try that you haven't yet?
3. What is your biggest regret?
4. What does a successful life look like to you?
5. My favorite way to spend the day is...
6. If I could talk to my teenage self, the one thing I would say is...
7. The two moments I'll never forget in my life are...
8. Using 30 words or less, describe yourself
9. What's one skill or strategy you need to learn more about to help you live a more fulfilling life?
10. Make a list of ten things you want to ask for but you never have. How would your life be different if you asked for these?

Supercharge Your
Resilience

"We can't become what we need to be by remaining what we are."

— **Oprah Winfrey**

According to the American Psychological Association, "Resilience is the process of adapting well in the face of adversity, trauma, tragedy, threats, or significant sources of stress", such as family and relationship problems, health issues, or a financial crisis.

A person that has mastered the art of resilience can bounce back from difficult experiences. It is the ability to forge ahead through rough times, no matter what that is.

Are you going through a difficult experience or trauma right now? Are you questioning your commitment to pushing forward? Having doubt as to whether you can get over the next hurdle? Do you think about your breaking point, and what that could be?

Relax. You are stronger than you think. You are more courageous than you give yourself credit for. Your level of resilience is always the determining factor when it comes to winning over any challenge or obstacle.

Resilience is more than just a state of mind; it is a way of life. How you approach your challenges—and the attitude you have toward obstacles—plays a huge part in how you work through difficulties. By acknowledging the trauma or difficulty and accepting it into your life, you will become better equipped to handle it without losing your mind.

If you lack the capacity to deal with life's misfortunes, you will be hit hard when they happen. You might be tempted to flee, instead of fight, or hide, instead of inviting the challenge and giving it your all.

People with strong resilience can tap into their inner strength to work through even the most difficult circumstances. How much resilience you have is dependent on several factors, but regardless, the good news is you can develop your mind to become as strong as you want it to be.

Resilience isn't something you are born with; rather, it is something you are conditioned to have. People who are well-disciplined can persevere and show tremendous willpower when it comes to facing the raw adversity in their lives.

You can condition both your mind and body to get through anything. When many would fail, you will persevere. When many would give up and fall back, you will push on and break through. When the rest of the crowd fails, you will rise and succeed.

Resilience is the absolute belief that, no matter the impossible odds or circumstances, you are destined to win. Resilience will remove the obstacles that add stress and suffering to your life. No matter what happens, you will stick with it, persevere, grind it out, and be ready and willing to stand tall when everyone else is telling you to pack it in.

If you play sports, work in a tough business, or struggle with a debilitating illness, your level of resilience determines your ability to make it through to the other side. If you win or lose it doesn't make a difference. What matters is you gave it your all till the end.

Seven Ways to Empower Resiliency

If you've spent time working out, you know it takes time to build up strong muscles. You have to keep doing your sets and reps on a consistent basis. Apply this habit over the course of the weeks, months, and years ahead, and you will become unbeatable in the gym.

Now, apply that same mindset to building up resiliency. You need to realize that, no matter what, winning is a matter of forming a strong mindset, developed through consistent conditioning. You need to build the right frame of mind to take on everything pushing back against you.

Stop using negative excuses such as, "The world isn't fair," or "I never get a break." Nobody said it was fair, and fairness is a game for people who want it the easy way. You will always be on the receiving end of defeat if you wait on the world to favor the perfect circumstances.

Now, let's dive into the strategies you can apply to build up your resilience.

1. Remove "disaster thinking".

The greatest self-defeating force in all of us can be traced back to our thoughts. Just one negative thought can cause everything else to fall like dominoes. For example, obsessive thoughts that focus on worry creates an easy path for scarcity thinking to take over your mind.

You start thinking that no matter what, you have less, and everyone else has more. This leads to deeper fears about the future. If you have less now, won't you have less in the future, too? Of course you will. Scarcity thinking attaches itself to your brain and literally takes over. From there, all sorts of fears start to grow.

Worry and fear are like two twisters that funnel into a bigger storm. Disaster thinking always begins with a belief that the worst is yet to come. You believe all your efforts are doomed to fail anyway, so why bother?

However, you can defeat this right now by accepting this truth: Change, sickness, and death are the only constants in life that are inevitable. These events will happen. Why worry about events that ultimately happen anyway? Now, you can see the way to become great.

More people are defeated by their own thoughts than anything else. Thought affects everything else, too. It either turns your mindset into a powerful ally, or a fearful one. It either makes you stand up for more or knocks you down.

Resilient people think differently than the 97% of people who are controlled by confusion and chaos. When you are focused on being resilient, you know that, no matter what negativity is out there trying to break its way in, it won't topple your positive mindset.

You can crush any negative thought that enters your mind. After all, the reason it is there in the first place is because you gave it the power to grow. You give your thoughts power, and you can take it away, too.

Focus on your thinking and observe when it spirals out of control. Bring it back and train your thoughts to stay focused in the present moment.

2. Do something now.

It is easy to put off doing tasks you have a strong resistance to. We want the conditions to be right for the cause. We don't want to act until we have trained more, studied more, or built up our confidence and courage. We wait until we are fully equipped to handle the situation, but instead of acting, we waste time preparing for battle.

Yet, we never actually go to war.

It is true we have to prepare ourselves in advance for the challenges that lie ahead of us. However, look at the smaller actions you can take while you are preparing yourself for the big game.

One area that defeats us again and again is putting off until tomorrow what can be done today. The problem is, someday eventually arrives, and by that time, we realize it is too late.

Now is the only time that matters. Now is when the greatest impact can be made.

To overcome the habit of procrastination and focus on performing at peak levels throughout the day, I use a hundred-year-old strategy called "the Ivy Lee Method". It only takes a few minutes a day to set up, and it can change everything about the way you manage your personal productivity.

It works like this:

1. At the end of each workday, write down the six most important things you need to accomplish tomorrow. Do not write down more than six tasks.
2. Prioritize those six items in order of their true importance.

3. When you arrive tomorrow, concentrate only on the first task. Work until the first task is finished, before moving on to the second task.
4. Approach the rest of your list in the same fashion. At the end of the day, move any unfinished items to a new list of six tasks for the following day.
5. Repeat this process every morning.

"The world breaks everyone, and afterward, some are strong at the broken places."

— **Ernest Hemingway**

3. Be inspired by the greatness of others.

There are many stories of people who have faced incredible odds and survived. There are many who faced the same challenges and didn't make it through. For instance, take Viktor Frankl, who spent years in a Nazi death camp, enduring the worst way of life imaginable. How did Viktor survive, and so many others failed? Was it just luck or fate?

Perhaps both, but on a deeper level, Viktor knew to survive, he needed to see life beyond the camp, after the war. He would imagine delivering a presentation to people on what happened, and how he survived. He also thought of his wife, whom he later learned had died in another camp.

As Frankl stated: "We can't always change the circumstances thrust upon us, but we can change our attitude towards it." One of the key factors of resilience is attitude. Your attitude toward overcoming an obstacle is always the greatest tool you can focus on in any given situation.

Is there a story that inspires you to keep going when you feel like giving up? Is there someone in this world you look up to as a role model, whose message drives you to win? If there is, learn everything you can about this person. How do they do what they do? What traits make this person great?

Ask yourself: "How could my life change if I started to model this person's style? Where would I be a year from now by implementing just one of their strategies?"

Through modeling another person's belief system, habits, words, and even their body movements we can change how we think, act and feel. Take a habit that you are weak at and find someone who is succeeding where you are struggling. Find out everything you can about what they do to stay on top.

You can change anything in your life; your beliefs about money, the way you manage your health, and how you spend the first hour of every morning.

Observe the greatness of others and blaze your own trail by modeling what worked for them.

4. Abandon the obsession to change the situation.

Do you find yourself questioning the events or circumstances by asking yourself, "Why did this happen to me?" It is natural to fall into the victim role. Things were going so well, and now, you are on the opposite side of the fence, wondering, "What happened?".

Here is an example: Two years ago, a friend of mine, whom I'll call George, had it all: A wife whom he loved, and a good job. Then, one day, it all changed. Circumstances beyond his control left him without a job, and when he turned to his wife for emotional support during this difficult time, she left to find someone else who had a better-paying job and security.

From having everything to losing so much, George sank into a depression, but during this difficult time, he was also no stranger to hardships. After growing up in poverty and having to fight for most things in his life, George could tap into that strength again to pull himself through the pain he was experiencing.

He remembered something his father had said to him one day:

"If you let the people, places, and circumstances decide your fate, you'll always be defeated by other people's decisions and behavior. So, put your life in the best hands possible… your own."

George realized he could get another job, and there were more people out there he could connect with, who would be even better than the connections he had before. George focused on making a better future. Within three months, he went from zero to hero again, securing a better job and meeting someone else, who turned out to be his soulmate.

The reality is, life gives us some big challenges. What matters are not the cards you were dealt, but how you play that hand. In the moment of your life's greatest storm, you can be the solid tree that stands against the bad weather.

People who lose when life gets hard end up whining and complaining to anyone who will listen. They say things like, "Why did this happen to me?" or "Nothing ever works out, so why bother."

If you think that way, you put a mindset in motion that is destined to fail you. Catch yourself when you take the road to self-pity. Resilience begins with refusing to give in to your troubles.

Did someone dump you, and you're feeling rejected? Get out there and connect with people who love you. Did the business you've been working on for the past year go bankrupt? Take a break and set up a new business plan. Are you overweight, and do you hate looking at yourself in the mirror? Stop looking in the mirror, get off the scale, and get on a healthy diet that works.

Learn from what went wrong and try it again—without the same mistakes this time. Resilient people are fighters. They achieve greatness because they are great on the inside.

You have two choices: You can either push through your greatest challenge, or... don't. You choose to win or lose. The decision is always yours.

5. Tell yourself these three words: "It is possible."

Three of the most powerful words you can repeat to yourself right now are these: "It is possible." Resilient people, who continue to show up and play the game— even after they've failed—know the success of achieving their goal means showing up to play the game in the first place.

The odds may be against you, you may be outmatched, or people may tell you what you are trying to do just isn't possible or hasn't been done before. History is filled with the stories of people who succeeded, despite the odds stacked against them. Sometimes, they didn't achieve the objective they set out to achieve, but they hit a different mark altogether.

When you stay resilient, you maintain the mindset and belief that all things are possible. Every situation can be understood, any defeat can be turned around. When someone tells you something is impossible, remember what they mean is it is impossible for them, but not for you.

The minute you commit to the "impossibility", you set the standard for everything else down the pipeline. You want to win at a sport? Impossible. You want to write a book? Can't do it. You want to quit your job? Not now. Believing with all your heart that whatever you want to achieve now can be done is the game-changer in making it really happen.

Look at Richard Bannister, who broke the record for running one mile in under four minutes. They said it couldn't be done, but he was resilient and trained hard for months, both physically and psychologically. He trained himself to believe it was possible, and his goal could be achieved—even when he was surrounded by people who claimed it could not be done—and on May 6, 1954, he broke the record at 3:59.

Impossibilities can become real possibilities if we believe in them. When you believe in something so strongly that you're unwilling to accept anything else but the result you want, you are tapping into your greatest source of power. The Undefeated exist here.

6. Set a Big Goal.

For years I didn't like who I was. After believing the voices of critics, I had a hard time believing in what I could achieve. So, when it came to setting goals, I would aim low... and hit the mark every time.

Goals are positive indicators of your success. If you are working on something that could have a significant impact on your life, you will be excited, passionate, and enthusiastic to work on it. You should create goals that are larger than life, and not built on the limited beliefs of what the world tells you is possible.

Resilient people are adept at knocking down goals, whereas many others have no goals to speak of. By achieving goals many would consider to be "too difficult" or even "impossible", you are increasing your level of resilience beyond what many people will ever achieve. By doing this consistently over months and years, you will become unbreakable.

So, ask yourself this question: Is there a life goal you have been holding onto? Something you've never shared with anyone? Something that scares you so badly that thinking about it makes you sweaty with anxiety? A dream so big that people call you crazy to be even thinking about it?

You might think I'm exaggerating, but unless your goal scares you—unless it is so big that it appears impossible—then chances are, you won't be fulfilled by aiming low. You have to be willing to fail big—or else you will just fail.

7. Experience everything and welcome the fear.

Experience is a great teacher. You want to experience as much of this life as you can. Instead of holding back, charge forward. Instead of setting limits, become limitless in your approach. Instead of saying, "I'll do it later," do it now. Instead of waiting for someone else to act first, you act first.

Resilience is not a gift, but a reward. It is what you have after years of trying and failing, pushing ahead, and taking it on the chin. It is what you gain by doing all this while you are scared. Resilience is a gift to yourself that you can later teach others to build up.

Adapt to the ongoing changes and drop the complaining habit. Complaining holds you back and steals your ability to do something about the situation. Do you know anyone who has made a difference by complaining incessantly about a situation they can't control? It weakens you and sets you up for failure.

Be resilient by avoiding the habits that make you weak and empower the actions that make you strong.

Supercharge Your
Focus

"I don't focus on what I'm up against. I focus on my
goals and I try to ignore the rest."

— Venus Williams

Success in anything is dependent on the strength of
your focus. This isn't about all the distractions we have
these days. The truth is, people were just as distracted
100 years ago. They just had different distractions.

Deep focus begins with your mind. Concentration is a
laser-focused skill that can get more work done in two
hours than most people get done in a full day. With
deep focus laser-sighted on what you want, distraction
isn't an issue.

Focus is the trained ability to say NO to the distractions
of television, chatter, or senseless news that fights for
your attention.

Focus is powerful when you are engaged in deep work.
This skill takes time to develop. But time is what you
have. So here is how you can master focus:

Schedule your deep focus time. Deep focus isn't a zone
you live in all day. It must be intentional. People who

can focus for long periods of time built up to this through practice. You should schedule time for focusing until you can do it for longer periods of time.

Build your deep-focus environment. The space you live in, work or do deep thinking plays a role in your deep focus. If you're surrounded by external noise, pets, children, or a constant influx of noise, it will be hard to focus for any length of time. It's important to be clear on where you plan to practice deep focus. When you have your space set up, you have to...

Prepare your mind. Before diving in, take ten minutes to warm up your internal engines. Listen to a piece of focusing music or soothing ambience. Breathe deeply for five minutes. Think about what you're working on today. Visualize the road you are building. See the bridge to your freedom as you show up each day to do the work.

Know what you're focusing on. I was a master multi-tasker. But I had low results to show for it. I would start a new task every ten minutes and be exhausted after 2 hours. This is what happens when you try to do everything and continue to transition from task to task. It wears you down.

If you work on a computer, get rid of all the open tabs. You only need to be looking at what you're focusing on. Time is a valuable resource. The work you are committed to must be worthy of your time. If not, it isn't what you should be spending deep focus on.

What will you focus on in this moment?

Begin your deep focus session. Set your timer for 30-45 minutes. I suggest starting with 30 minutes if this is your first time to plan your focus. You are training your brain to focus at a time when it is scheduled and not just when it feels like it.

For many people, we let our brain decide when to work, take breaks, or go off on a completely different tangent. By scheduling it in, you are training your brain to work according to your schedule and not a random time of day when the mood is right.

Block Your Time in 15-Minute Increments

Time is a valuable resource. It's more valuable than money because it cannot be replaced. Once your time is gone; it's gone forever. Who has time to waste on mind-numbing tasks when we could be doing what we love? But it isn't that easy when there is so much to do at once.

Monkey Mind lives for this. It wants you to multitask and do as much or as little as you can. This is why I started breaking my time into 15-minute sessions.

Use a timer and set it for 15 minutes. Decide what you are going to work on for 15 minutes.

Will you:

- Meditate?
- Start writing a blog post?
- Send an email that you've been putting off?
- Listen to a piece of classical music?

The purpose is to discipline your mind to stick with a habit. In this case, a habit of working within a short amount of time. By limiting this habit to just 15 minutes, you are not overcommitting or stressing out about not acting.

Write down how you will focus for your 15-minute session:

Focus on Just One Task

Multitasking doesn't work, and you are no more productive when working on several things at the same time. To be really effective, your mind can accomplish anything if it focuses on just one task at a time.

If you are working on a project that has multiple steps and will take several months to complete, break it down into sub-steps and mini actions.

Plan your actions ahead and know what you are working on, and then commit to this one action for the allocated time.

Be Aware of Your Anxiety

One reason we get distracted is because we lose touch with our emotional program. When you feel bored, you want to be entertained. When you are feeling fearful, you would rather be distracted in order to deal with the fear.

Anxiety creates fearful thinking. And, if you are a nervous or fearful person, you have more anxiety than others. When I get anxious, I get restless and bored. I look for something to fix me and this could lead to poor choices.

When this happens, you can calm yourself down by listening to a favorite piece of music or practice deep breathing. I would recommend NOT turning on the TV or using the computer during your times of anxiety.

Make a list of 3—5 thoughts or activities that make you anxious:

Mind-numbing activities will help you escape, but those same emotions are still there looking for some stillness to their existence. Mastering your emotions is an amazing form of self-control.

Learning to direct your actions and not just doing something habitually will put you in greater control of your own life and choices.

I recommend that you:

1. Read a chapter from a book. Try Stillness Speaks by Eckhart Tolle or Fear: Essential Wisdom for Getting Through the Storm by Thich Nhat Hanh.
2. For music, check out "Weightless" by Marconi Union. This song is considered to be one of the most relaxing songs in the world. It has done wonders for my anxiety moments.
3. Meditate. Just put yourself in a place of quiet calmness and use the 15-minute-block technique. Play a song while meditating and relax. If you need some suggestions for meditation, check out Meditation for Beginners: 20 Practical Tips for Understanding the Mind by Leo Babauta.
4. Read positive quotes and affirmations to yourself. Yes, quotes are powerful enough to put your mind in a relaxed state. They can raise your energy level and put your mind in a positive state.

After practicing one of the above activities, write out your thoughts about the emotional effect it has on your thinking. Is your mind clear? Do you feel peaceful? Are you less anxious?

Start Keeping a Goals Journal

I've talked about the importance of goals several times in this book, so you know how serious I am about creating a goal. Keeping a goals journal is a great first step.

This is a journal for keeping track of the goals you are working on, notes about progress, and challenges along the way. You can fill up your journal with positive quotes and affirmations as well.

At the end of the day, spend a few minutes reading through your journal. Prioritize the mini tasks you are working on, so you will know that you are working on something. Create a checklist of your goals and set up daily tasks. Schedule time every morning or evening to write something in your journal.

I added a new goal every day—even if it was a small one. After six months, I had over 200 written down. If you want to distract your mind, divert your attention toward setting and working toward these goals.

What is your #1 goal for this week? This month?

Action

Set up a time block for your focus session. This can be 15, 30 or 45 minutes. I recommend the shorter time when starting out. Decide before hand what you will focus on.

You can spend this time working, mediating or focusing on just your thoughts. Increase your focus time by five minutes every week and try to build up to 60 minutes.

Focus on Becoming Clutter-Free

"Always remember, your focus determines your reality."

— George Lucas

One key practice that is guaranteed to sharpen your focus is managing the "clutter of things" in your environment. This includes both at work and at home. Clutter in your space can pull your focus away as you become aware of the things on shelves, under your feet and taking up space on your desk, or in the corner of your room.

You should make a goal to live a clutter-free lifestyle. Living a clutter-free lifestyle is about three things: 1. Wanting less, 2. Getting rid of your excess items around the house, and 3. Managing your negative thoughts taking up space in your mind.

Instead of gathering more things, a clutter free lifestyle focuses on creating quality life experiences, and enjoying the finer things in life that don't cost money. Living without clutter in your life is a choice you can make.

You begin by getting rid of the extra stuff around your home that takes up space but has no useful purpose.

You can start by cleaning out the garage or your living room. Give away the things you don't need to friends or recycle through selling to recycle shops.

"The process of assessing how you feel about the things you own, identifying those that have fulfilled their purpose, expressing your gratitude, and bidding them farewell, is really about examining your inner self, a rite of passage to a new life."

— Marie Kondo

To live clutter free requires a shift in your habits and mindset. For example, stop buying items online you don't need. When you go shopping, don't buy something unless it is a necessity. By reducing clutter, you can save money and gain more freedom by living in a clean and clutter-free space.

Begin the decluttering habit by tracking what you spend money on every day. This is a difficult habit to begin, but if you stick with it for 30 days, it will become a part of your daily routine.

You can start tomorrow by tracking your expenses. At the end of the week, add everything up and consolidate expenses. What did you buy that has the potential to become clutter later? Did you buy this on impulse, or is it a necessity?

There are 4 key benefits to creating a clutter-free life:

1. Reduced stress because you're not constantly in pursuit of owning more things.

2. Less living space required. With a clutter-free lifestyle, we need less room for things. This adds to a cleaner living space and eliminates the need to be constantly cleaning around your stuff.

3. Improved focus. With less stress and less stuff, you can increase your focus. Better focus leads to greater productivity in your life.

4. A Greater sense of joy and freedom. You have freedom from collecting things. We become attached to possessions and build a false sense of self-worth by what we own. You can be genuine while living a life of freedom with less to collect and worry about keeping.

Living clutter-free will give you more time, energy, and more money to spend on trips with family.

Here are 5 simple steps you can start with to build your clutter-free lifestyle.

1. Spend a weekend to declutter your home. You can sell your things, throw it or give it away.

2. Start with each room and move through your house decluttering as you go.

3. Take old clothes to the used clothing shops. Take your books to libraries or used books stores.

4. If you have a home office, declutter your workspace. Identify clutter and get rid of it.

5. Browse fewer shopping sites online or stop this habit completely. By looking at shopping every day, you become tempted to buy stuff.

Action Step

Look around your home and collect things you no longer need. You can sell, give away or recycle these items. Make it a goal to reduce your stuff by at least 50%.

Work on one room at a time by doing a room per week—or day—depending on how much stuff you have.

Use a checklist for each room as you move through and declutter everything:

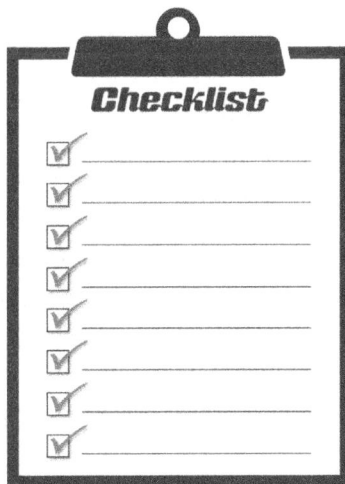

Create a Productive Workspace

It is a very satisfying feeling to have a home that is clutter-free. But what about your work space? Can you work efficiently if your space is covered with junk, papers, files, and stationary?

Many work stations can become very disorganized and cluttered during the working day when we are busy on projects, meetings or rushing to meet a deadline.

Office and desk clutter create chaos, not only in our working environment but, in your mind as you lose things and waste valuable work time looking for stuff.

There are 4 reasons to keep a clean workspace:

It increases productivity. The less time you spend trying to find documents, papers and stationary, the more time you can spend focusing on work that matters. Knowing where your files and documents are gives you greater control and access to documents while keeping your office clean.

It presents a professional atmosphere. Keeping your office space clean not only gives a better representation, but it's also a way of showing that you are a working professional who cares about their work. A messy office space can't be taken seriously, and it is very demotivating.

It creates a calming mindset. Chaos is impossible to work in. Clutter affects your mental space and drains your mind of energy fast. When your mind is thinking about the condition of your office, you tend to be distracted and lack the focus and concentration needed. A cluttered office is a representation of a cluttered mind.

Here are 3 simple tips to keep a clutter free workstation.

Go digital. You know all those papers, notebooks and files you have around your desk and in drawers? Create digital files for these things and digitize your documents by creating electronic copies, either by scanning them or typing them out instead. You can keep all your digital material in cloud or Google Docs

Create the habit of organizing. The best habit you can create to stay clutter-free is to develop a new habit of cleanliness and organization. Whenever a new item is introduced into the office, decide what you plan to do with it at that moment.

Where will you keep it? Preventing the clutter of items we use daily is the best way to keep your work space clean.

Clean up before you leave. When it's time to go home, take the last ten minutes of your day to clean your desk and work space. Put away things that are not where they should be. This will make your workday for tomorrow much smoother when you come into work with a clean station to start with.

In the space below, write down how you feel after decluttering your workspace. Do you notice a. difference in your thoughts? If you do, your thinking is clearer. You're no longer thinking about the clutter that is running your life.

Take a photo of your office space now. Then, commit to cleaning your space for the next week. Take a photo at the end and see the difference your decluttering has made.

Photographs provide a different perspective, and potential problems could be seen from the picture, helping you identify the areas that need to be cleaned up regularly.

For a deeper dive into how to master your focus, check out my book **Empower Your Deep Focus**.

Supercharge Your
Beliefs

"Believe in yourself! Have faith in your abilities!
Without a humble but reasonable confidence in
your own powers, you cannot be successful or
happy."

— **Norman Vincent Peale**

Beliefs play a pivotal role in shaping the course of your life. But, beliefs are not set in stone. We can change some of our core beliefs if we implement a specific process. When your old beliefs fail you, and the same script is used to run your life without change, it's time to take intentional action and create a new story for yourself.

You are responsible for the beliefs you choose to create. Regardless of what you have been taught, you are in control of your own state of mind (aka mindset). With the right tools and guidance, there is nothing in your life that cannot be created or reinvented. Now, let's take a look at making some changes in your belief system.

You should consider changing your beliefs if they:

- No longer support your current goals, dreams, and mission.
- Feed into and support negative thoughts and destructive behavior.
- Limit your potential for success.
- Prevent you from taking action toward the fulfillment of your great purpose.

We can all make changes in regard to our beliefs. Some of these beliefs are easy to spot, resting in plain sight on the surface. Others are less obvious and require a deeper level of insight and acute awareness. As you work on altering these beliefs, you will start to notice changes in your own physiology.

Emotionally, you will start to feel better about who you are. Physically, you will feel stronger and look better. Mentally, you will be more focused on your needs, as well as on the needs of others.

But, the beliefs I am concerned about are those that confine my potential. The beliefs that funnel my vision into a narrow funnel and severely limit my chances to lead an extraordinary life. Self-limiting beliefs blame someone —or everyone—for how life has turned out.

It builds on resentment and loves to spin negative thought cycles around continuously with no chance of escape. If your beliefs—and coexisting thoughts—are keeping you prisoner, now is the time to create a break-free strategy.

How to Change Your Limiting Beliefs: The Six-Step Process

Believe it or not, you can change a belief in an instant. The challenge is in recognizing the beliefs that should be switched so they are in alignment with your current values and needs.

It is important to understand that beliefs have created the circumstances in our lives. When we change something, we can change the circumstances. This is one way to experience a transformation. In almost every case, this requires the following changes:

1. An individual must change their beliefs about something.

2. And they must change the thoughts supporting those beliefs.

Here are six steps you can take to begin changing anything in your life. Keep in mind that this takes time and you won't always succeed by doing something once or twice. Like any habit, you have to keep at it.

Step 1: Identify the belief you want to change. This is the first step to taking positive action. You can only change something if you know what you need to change, and why you want to change it.

Core negative beliefs that make you feel inferior, inadequate, or worthless should be first on your list. Why hang on to your painful thoughts any longer? This is a tough step for most people. We have been feeding into our pain for so long it starts to appear normal.

I can assure you that in working through your pain, and recognizing the negative beliefs you created about yourself, your life will begin to take a dramatic shift.

Here are some examples of beliefs you may have about yourself. See if you recognize any of these:

"Everything bad that happens to me is my fault."

"I feel like I am less competent than everyone else when it comes to success or getting ahead in life."

"I feel like a failure or a 'nobody' when in the presence of other people who are obviously better than me."

"I have no qualities worth talking about that anyone would be interested in."

"I should be perfect at all times. I have to show people I am perfect."

"I am inherently flawed."

"I am inferior. Everyone else is smarter, more educated, and they seem to land on their feet when all I do is fail from day to day."

"I'm no good, and everyone knows it."

"Once someone gets to know me, they will just leave me like everyone else."

"My family was extremely dysfunctional; so, I am dysfunctional."

"If only she would stop treating me that way, I'd feel better about this situation and myself."

You might have a number of faulty beliefs about yourself that have disempowered you throughout most of your life. I know I did before I worked to turn them around. The key is to recognize what they are. Some are buried deep. Others are more noticeable and are running through your mind a hundred times a day. They feel so normal that you don't question their validity.

Take time to write them out and list as many as you can. You can start with parts of the short list above that apply and add to it with your own negative beliefs. Pay attention to the beliefs that target your self-esteem and devalue your worth.

You can replace your negative belief with positive expressions. Here are a few examples:

- I am living a significant life
- I have everything I need to succeed
- I'm living my dream right now
- Nothing can stop me from getting what I want

Step 2: Disempower the old belief by injecting doubt and uncertainty. It is time to take a stand and question your belief thoroughly, analyzing it under a mental microscope through strict analysis. It is time to put your beliefs on trial.

You are going to question your beliefs, attack their vulnerability, tear down their walls, and weaken their structure. If a belief has been built on lies and falsehoods, it will not stand up to the scrutiny of your attack.

Here is an example:

"My family was extremely dysfunctional; so, I am dysfunctional."

Begin by questioning this belief. Take away its power. Make a decision to reject it. Here's what I wrote.

"What is the basis for this belief?"

"My family life was not perfect by any means. My parents loved me conditionally and they had their own issues to deal with. Many times I felt rejected. But this doesn't mean I am dysfunctional. To a degree, isn't everyone? Don't we all struggle with our own defects? I refuse to accept this belief anymore."

Go deep with your ideas and push back hard. Then, ask pertinent questions that disengage the power your belief has over you. Put your belief on trial! Tell yourself that this is not a reality you choose to believe in anymore. Disown it completely. Choose to believe in something else. This is when your mind makes a shift toward reframing what it has been trained to accept.

Step 3: Reframe the new belief while discarding the old one. Full of fear, self-doubt, and lacking confidence, we can easily slip back into old patterns of defeat. We can convince ourselves that negative beliefs are true.

When you decide to replace your old beliefs, you are making a firm commitment: I refuse to feel this way anymore. From now on, I am going to reject all negative thoughts. If you do this enough, you will be thinking and behaving differently.

Step 4: Visualize the person you will become once you have created a new belief. Visualize yourself behaving differently, taking new and decisive actions, and pushing through your fear instead of being blocked by it. See yourself overcoming the obstacles that, until now, have been holding you back. Imagine the new way of life that waits for you on the other side of conquering your fears.

Then, visualize the steps that you would need to take to make this transition. What could you do right now to begin building momentum? How would you have to think and act to achieve an outcome that is seemingly beyond your reach or capability? Once you have the clear answer, it is time to start being that person.

Step 5: Reinforce the new belief, taking further repetitive action toward making it real. Now that you have a solid idea of the changes you want, start by supporting your new belief. Take immediate action and reframe your old belief with the new one.

If you tear down the old belief but do nothing to replace it, you'll eventually resort to that old destructive way of thinking. When this happens, just remember what your replacement belief is and continue to reinforce it over and over. Such reinforcement has to be done consistently in order to succeed.

Try writing out ten of your favorite quotes. Utilize the power of positive words and affirmations. Repeat these several times a day. It will be uncomfortable at first, but be persistent.

The more you use words of positive power, the faster you can shift your beliefs to accepting what you are saying and thinking. Persistence and consistency are the keys. Soon you will be able to pull out your positive mental toolbox and use it to overpower negative thoughts and words.

Self-conversation is a powerful tool. Your negative beliefs used this tool against you for many years. Now you know that you can choose thoughts that support your new belief. Give your new belief lots of encouragement and support. Repeat it as many times as you need to. Convince yourself that it is true!

Step 6: Follow-up with action. In this final stage, you are going to continually strengthen your belief through convincing evidence. You will alter your actions and behaviors to align with the new belief as it starts planting roots deep in your subconscious.

It is important to continually reinforce new beliefs. Check in with yourself regularly and clear your mind of the trash. I think of this as "deleting" the trash, just like you would on your desktop.

Action Step

- You must continuously work to reinforce your new beliefs. Create the beliefs you want to have and do not settle on thoughts that devalue you.
- Be aware of the negative beliefs you cling to, and develop a unique approach by using positive phrases.

- Create the beliefs you want to have. Do not settle on thoughts that devalue you.

Beliefs set the standard for everything that is possible in your life. They are the powerful engines of certainty and deep-rooted convictions. If you want to be the force that controls your own destiny, you must learn to control your beliefs. They have the power to build you up or ruin you.

The reality you live in reflects what you believe. If you are happy and prosperous, with a positive outlook and attitude, it is because you are engaging in an empowering belief system that has created this way of life.

Beliefs are incredibly persuasive, continuously shaping the course of our lives. You can dictate the beliefs that guide your life. You can choose to believe that good things are happening all around you, or you can choose not to believe in anything and take your chances.

You are responsible for the beliefs you choose to create. Regardless of what you have been taught, you are in control of your own state of mind. With the right tools and guidance, there is nothing in your life that cannot be created or reinvented. Now, let's take a look at making some changes in our belief system.

Thoughts Shapes Beliefs. The experiences we have create many of our beliefs. If those experiences were perceived as frightful or harmful, we develop a phobia surrounding the fear to try to avoid repeating that experience at all costs.

Everyone has something they fear, and this fear begins with your belief in something that is harmful, dangerous, or a threat.

Remember that what you believe in becomes your reality. If you believe in the fears that govern your life and control your actions, this is the reality you create for yourself. The things you positively believe in are attracted to you.

The things you fear the most are also attracted to you. Change your fear-based beliefs and you can shift the possible negative outcome of any situation into a positive experience.

What outcome do you want to experience?

Challenge the beliefs holding you prisoner. The most fearful events of all are imagined ones. We imagine over and over again the terrifying events that are going to take place.

We obsess about them, think about them, and try to invent ways that will stop the worst from coming true by avoiding all risks whatsoever. In the process, many of us end up avoiding living our lives once the fear becomes so bad.

Inevitably, you are creating the situations allowing these disasters to occur. Remember, most fear is an illusion of disbelief that we are convinced is the truth.

This is how fear starts to build itself up. It starts as something small at one point, and through the habitual practice of consistent fear building, events that never take place blossom into uncontrollable fantasies of terror.

Take charge and challenge your irrational beliefs and thoughts. Think about what would happen if the worst event imaginable really did occur. Often it is not the fear of what will happen that scares us the most; rather, it is the doubt of our own ability to handle the situation when and if it does happen. We are afraid of ourselves, afraid that we won't be able to find a solution to deal with a fearful situation when it happens.

The way you think has a strong influence on your quality of life. This is especially true when it comes to the power of beliefs. The power of your beliefs determines if you are living a limited lifestyle or a limitless one.

The beliefs you feed your mind are the beliefs you design your life with.

If your beliefs are not supporting your dreams or goals, it's time to change the old system and replace it with supportive thoughts that help you to succeed.

What is the #1 belief that is holding you back now?

Your mindset is not permanent—it can always be changed if you have the courage to change it. And you have the courage to do anything you want!

If you are still holding onto limiting beliefs about yourself that have disempowered you throughout most of your life, you can change them from today.

You should replace limiting beliefs with positive messages about who you really want to become. Here are a few affirmations to get you started:

- I am living a great life.

- I have everything I need to succeed.

- I'm living my dream right now.

- Nothing can stop me from getting what I want.

Beliefs have created the circumstances in your life. When you change your beliefs, you change your perspective of the surrounding circumstances. This is how people experience a transformation.

Remember that you are always in control of your own state of mind. You can challenge the beliefs holding you back.

Here are the six steps you just learned so you can begin forming new beliefs:

1. Step 1: Identify the belief you want to change.

2. Step 2: Disempower the old belief by injecting doubt and uncertainty.

3. Step 3: Reframe the new belief while discarding the old one.

4. Step 4: Visualize the person you will become once you have created a new belief.

5. Step 5: Reinforce the new belief, taking further repetitive action toward making it real.

6. Step 6: Evaluate your beliefs on a regular basis.

It is important to reinforce your new beliefs on a continual basis. Create the beliefs you want to have and do not settle on thoughts that devalue you.

Analyze where you are at with your beliefs, and whether they are consistent with your desires and purpose.

Adopting a set of empowering beliefs is a key stepping stone to bringing change into your life. It triggers the law of attraction to action and soon you will witness the universal coincidences taking place in your life.

Creating Positive Affirmations

Create Positive Belief Affirmations to reinforce your beliefs. This is how you retrain your brain to think differently.

Here are 6 affirmations you can put into practice. At the end of this workbook you will find a "best list" of quotes filled with wisdom and ageless philosophy.

- I can do anything when my belief is strong enough

- I believe in my talents and skills to make things better wherever I go.

- Success is happening now; the future is not yet here. I will believe in the present moment as it is shaping my life for all the good stuff to come.

- Right now, I am transforming my beliefs for my own betterment.

- I am observing my past beliefs and releasing those beliefs which no longer bring joy, peace or happiness.

- I'm creating powerful and motivating thoughts that exceed all limiting beliefs.

Do you have a favorite affirmation to practice this week?

Raise Your Standards

Raising your standards means to set the value for how you are treated in this world. You determine what you are willing to accept from people, and they treat you according to the expectations you determine. For people that express low self-esteem and confidence, they allow themselves to be yelled at, bullied, and put down by people at work or in social gatherings.

If you don't set the standards for what you're willing to accept, the world will set those standards for you. You ultimately take control of your own life by drawing the line on what is acceptable and what you will tolerate.

You have to implement a level of standard for yourself. It's not the expectations of other people you should be paying attention to, but the expectations you have for yourself.

You turn your "should do" into a "must do." When you must get something done, you push yourself to do it. A should get it done becomes a someday goal that never gets accomplished.

How do you raise our standards?

By not accepting your limitations. Raise yourself to a level that challenges you in every area of your life. Determine your zero tolerance for what you'll accept.

Doing the work that is difficult but extremely rewarding. Surrounding yourself with people that have higher skillset or make 10x more money.

Avoiding excuses from yourself and staying away from complainers. You must raise your standards and become unlimited in your potential.

Your mind is a powerful thing. When you fill it with positive thoughts, your life will start to change.

Create the opportunity to get the job you want. Make friends with people that challenge you and raise you to their level where the winners are.

When you fail, you don't lower your standards to match the failure and make yourself feel better. You take your standards to the highest level.

When most people say NO, you are saying YES. Where 99% fail and give up, you are the 1% that pushes forward. You accept nothing but the absolute best, and your best is better than anyone else can commit to.

Commit yourself to becoming great at what you do. Then become the best at what you do, and become better than your best by aiming for mastery in your field.

Don't settle for good enough. Continue to close the gap on where you are to where you want to be. Fire your excuses and decide what you MUST do and not what you MIGHT do.

What MUST you do today? Tomorrow? Write down your thoughts:

Your potential will always reflect your standards. If your standards are average, your efforts will be average. This leads to average results. You can work 100 hours a week, but if you're working in a job you hate doing meaningless work it amounts to exhaustion and burnout. Success can only be reached when your standards are raised to a level that scares you.

Identify the fixed beliefs you have about yourself. Put in the work to change these beliefs in time. It won't happen right away, but if you identify your negative beliefs now, you make yourself aware of it.

What is your #1 negative belief right now?

You become what you believe, who you spend time with, and the self-talk communicated to yourself. You have control over these things. You can change your beliefs, spend time with real game winners, and change your limited self-talk.

Ask yourself:

- "What are the possibilities that become available when I raise my standards?"

- "What excuses are getting in my way?"

- "Where do I want to be emotionally, financially, and physically in five years from now?

Write down your answers here:

Model the Beliefs of Successful People

You can emulate the success of your mentors if you study the system of beliefs they used as a pathway toward personal excellence. Success breeds success, and beliefs can be passed on through a high level of instruction.

- Do you want to build financial freedom?
- Would you like to lose weight?
- Run your first marathon?
- Build your dream career?

Anything is possible when you follow the beliefs of those who've already achieved what you desire.

To be the person you want to become, start spending time with those who live the way you want to. Emulate their actions and behaviors, but—most importantly—model their beliefs and make them your own.

Successful people who accomplish great things in their lifetime have superior belief systems—beliefs that stretch to the unlimited pathways of excellence.

Who is your "hero", and what traits/skills do they have that you want to model?

Believe in "I Can"

When you believe you can, you definitely will. You build the mindset of a winner that becomes unstoppable.

Most of the wins we achieve in our lifetime has little to do with talent or skill.

It is the ability to create a vision for the life you truly desire. Then, following through with a set action plan to turn that vision into a reality.

When we tell ourselves that we can do it, this feeds in to the empowering belief that builds the possibility. If you tell yourself you can't, you will be right every time.

Only allow the finest thoughts to run within your mind on this journey of greatness.

Supercharge Your
Best Life Every Day

"If you have the courage to begin, you have the courage to succeed."

— David Viscott

The success strategies roadmap is the most important work you will do in your lifetime. It is a blueprint for the rest of your life. Don't wait for someone else to give you directions. You can start today with what you have, and take your first step towards a new existence. Only you can decide what that first step is.

People who fail to move forward are stuck in the road because they don't know what to do next, they don't know what direction to move in, and so they slide into performing self-defeating habits by default without awareness.

To begin your journey, you have to reset your day. Everyday. When you awaken, even before you get out of bed, you must seize your thoughts and direct this mental energy towards your vision, purpose, and goals. If you don't, the mind takes over quickly and can lead you down the wrong path before breakfast is over.

If you're afraid to take that first move, take it with confidence in knowing everybody is scared. The difference is, scared people move forward anyway. They don't let fear, doubt, uncertainty or procrastination get in the way.

In this module, the first step I introduced to you is Visualize Your Epic Life. If you want to have an Extraordinary Life, it begins today. There will never be a perfect time. If you wait, someday will turn into the next decade. Don't wait until it's too late. Regret is a pain you never want to experience as your last emotion.

Before we finish our time here together, I'll share with you a powerful story about Bronnie Ware, a palliative care nurse, whom sat by the bedside of many patients in their last days of living. During this time, many shared their heartbreaking regrets of a life never lived, dreams that never happened, and time that can never be returned.

One of the most common regrets shared by many was "I wish I'd had the courage to live a life true to myself, not the life others expected of me."

The best way to live a life is to plan your own path forward. You now have a powerful tool to show you the way. Don't hesitate to take action today. Build a life with joy, fulfillment and prosperity. Leave no regrets and at the end you will have lived a life worth living. This is the secret to success. But it begins with building the foundations.

The Master Plan Revisited

There is a lot to take in when it comes to building a great life. It can become overwhelming. This is why you have to take it one day at a time, one step at a time. Mastery is commitment to the steps, not perfecting the strategies in one week. You're on a journey, and this journey has no ending.

Remember the first lesson is to begin where you are. We are all at a different place on the map. Some people have made more progress than the rest of us, but that is okay. It is not a race, this is a marathon. You have no idea where your journey will take you. At first, you set out with a plan. It isn't a perfect plan, but it gets you moving.

As you push forward, your momentum creates opportunity that would never have appeared if you had done nothing. Massive action creates opportunity that is available to you only because of your commitment to the journey and passion to build your best life.

We can't predict the future. But we are creating it. I had no idea years ago when I boarded a plane with $500 in my pocket bound for Japan that I would experience a life of travel, excitement, and eventually, becoming a bestselling author. I've met thousands of people on this journey that have shaped and transformed everything in my life. And I hope that I influenced there life as well.

It began with a dream and a plan. That is all. From there, you have no idea what will transpire.

You have everything you need to get going. If you are still stuck, uncertain, or confused, go back to the beginning of this book and red through the strategies again. Take notes and focus in on your thoughts. Is negative thinking taking charge of your mind? Examine your beliefs. Do old beliefs still convince you this is impossible?

Visualize your life in one year, five or ten years from now. Are you still living the same life, or living in a way that feels impossible? My best advice: Take the impossible route. The Road Less Traveled is where you will discover everything you've ever dreamed of.

My dream and vision of what I aspire to achieve is to help 1,000,000 people discover their true awareness and live the life of their dreams. My thoughts, vision, and focus are laser-guided towards this dream. Will I succeed? I don't know for certain, but I do know this: If I stay committed to the path, lean into my uncertainty, and act no matter what while doing whatever it takes, I will change lives. It could be 1 million, or 10 million. It might be 5000. The number isn't important because each of you are worth so much more than you know.

When you're ready, let's begin...

 "A year from now you may wish you had started today."
— Karen Lamb

The excuses hold you back and you never actually start anything. If you want to start, you must begin. If you write nothing down on the blank page, it stays blank until you put pen to paper. Write one word. Just one. Then write another one. Make it a sentence.

You begin everything by taking that first step, no matter how easy it is. Make your decision to stop waiting and start doing. Turn off the TV. Move into silence and prepare your mind for what is coming.

It doesn't matter where you are at in your life right now, how much you've failed, or how hopeless your situation appears right now.

No matter where you are, who you are, how much you've failed in the past, you can start from where you're at. It's never too late to succeed or make tomorrow better than today, and today better than yesterday.

Procrastination is a fantasy that you can defeat with simple action tasks built into your routine. If procrastination is holding you back, and you're making excuses why you can't begin now, do the simplest thing imaginable.

Don't wait. You'll regret it. Begin your journey right now where you're at in this moment.

As Mark Twain once said, "The secret of getting ahead is getting started."

So, let's get started.

Begin where you are.

With what you have.

With who you are.

No time to waste.

It's time to begin.

Scott Allan

"Successful people do what unsuccessful people are not willing to do. Don't wish it were easier; wish you were better."

Jim Rohn

EMPOWER YOUR SUCCESS SERIES

BY SCOTT ALLAN

Available wherever books, eBooks and audiobooks are sold.

Bulletproof Mindset
Mastery Series

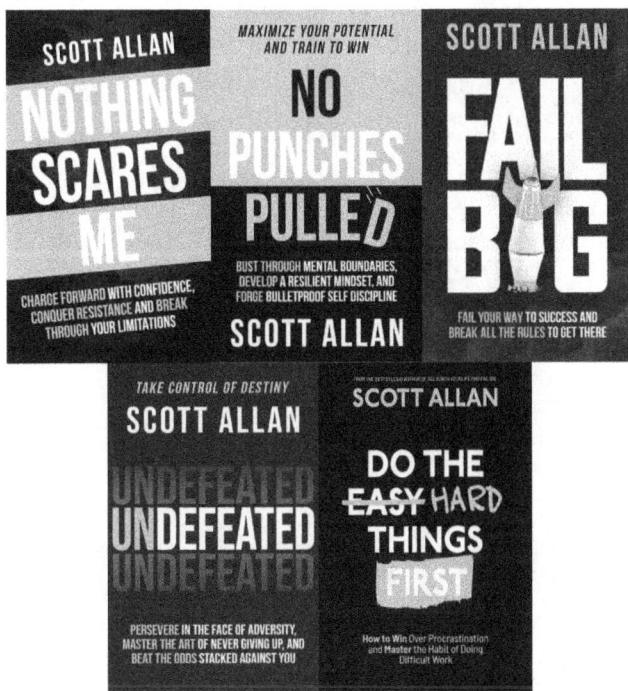

Available wherever books, eBooks and audiobooks are sold.

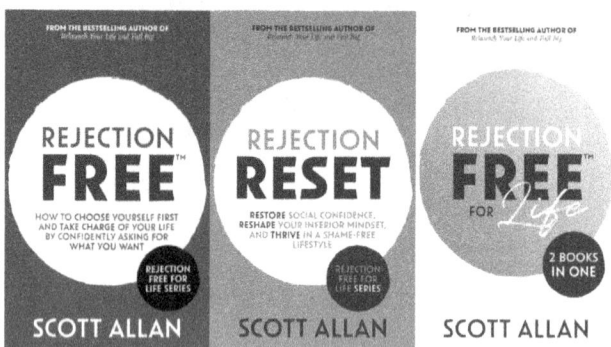

Available wherever books, eBooks and audiobooks are sold.

Break the Procrastination Habit, Accelerate Your
Productivity, and Take Control of Your Life NOW.

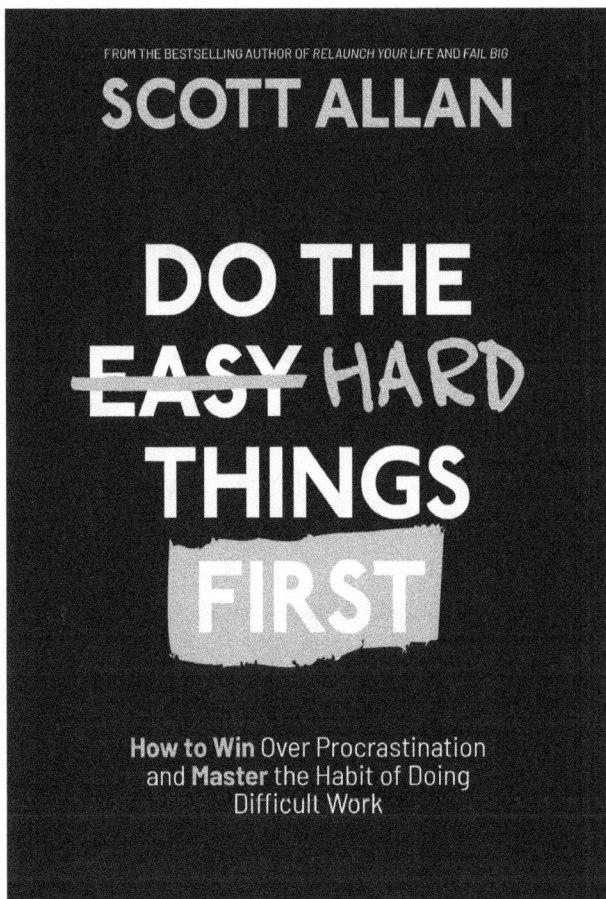

FROM THE BESTSELLING AUTHOR OF *RELAUNCH YOUR LIFE* AND *FAIL BIG*

SCOTT ALLAN

DO THE
~~EASY~~ HARD
THINGS
FIRST

How to Win Over Procrastination
and **Master** the Habit of Doing
Difficult Work

Available wherever books, eBooks and audiobooks are sold.

Bust Through Tough Obstacles, Develop a Resilient Mindset, and Forge Bulletproof Self Discipline

MAXIMIZE YOUR POTENTIAL AND TRAIN TO WIN

NO PUNCHES PULLED

BUST THROUGH MENTAL BOUNDARIES, DEVELOP A RESILIENT MINDSET, AND FORGE BULLETPROOF SELF DISCIPLINE

SCOTT ALLAN

Available wherever books, eBooks and audiobooks are sold.

ScottAllan SA
INTERNATIONAL

Conquer Imposter Syndrome, Develop a Resilient
Mindset, and Fail Forward With Confidence

Develop an Unbeatable Mindset, Transcend Difficult Obstacles, and Defeat Your Resistance to Change

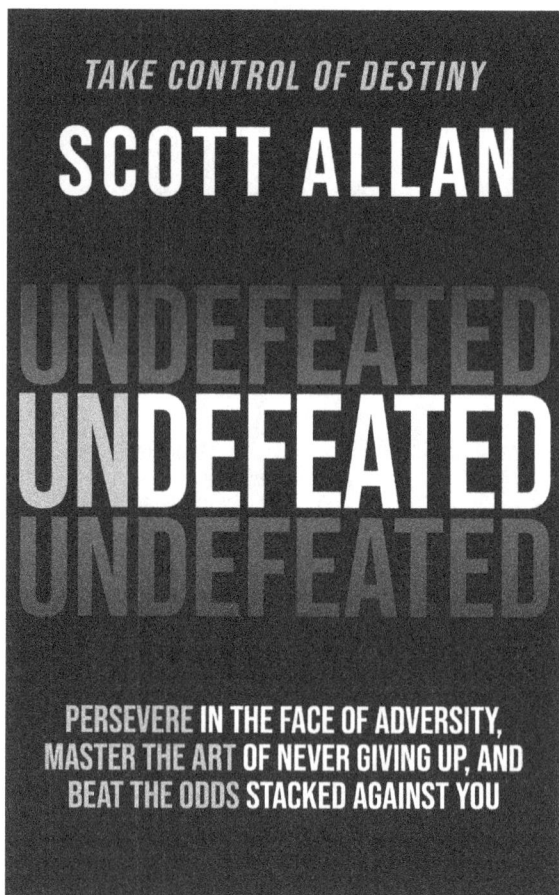

TAKE CONTROL OF DESTINY

SCOTT ALLAN

UNDEFEATED

PERSEVERE IN THE FACE OF ADVERSITY, MASTER THE ART OF NEVER GIVING UP, AND BEAT THE ODDS STACKED AGAINST YOU

Available wherever books, eBooks and audiobooks are sold.

EMPOWER YOUR
SUCCESS SERIES

BY SCOTT ALLAN

Available wherever books, eBooks and audiobooks are sold.

About Scott Allan

Scott Allan is an international bestselling author of 15+ books in the area of personal growth and self-development. He is the author of **Fail Big**, **Undefeated** and **Rejection Free**.

As a former corporate business trainer in Japan, and Transformational Mindset Strategist, Scott has invested over 10,000 hours of practice and research into the areas of self-mastery and leadership training.

With an unrelenting passion for teaching, building critical life skills, and inspiring people around the world to take charge of their lives, Scott Allan is committed to a path of constant and never-ending self-improvement.

Many of the success strategies and self-empowerment material that is reinventing lives around the world evolves from Scott Allan's 20 years of practice and teaching critical skills to corporate executives, individuals, and business owners.

You can connect with Scott at:

ScottAllan@scottallaninternational.com

Visit author.to/ScottAllanBooks **to stay up to date on future book releases.**

ScottAllan SA
INTERNATIONAL

www.ingramcontent.com/pod-product-compliance
Lightning Source LLC
Chambersburg PA
CBHW022049020426

42335CB00012B/606